**Iaroslav Wise**

# Cheer up!

Khmelnytskyi
Publisher Stasiuk L.S.
2019

УДК 821.111
В 14

There exist books dedicated to different topics such as how to use some software, how to learn to knit, how to operate a vehicle, etc. All of them teach particular skills. Few books, however, teach an attitude to start and accomplish any task. This book does just that. Whether you are building a house, studying or working, - you can find something useful in this book to help you accomplish your task.

**Вайз Я.**

В 14 Радійте! – Хмельницький, Видавець ФО-П Стасюк Л.С., 2019. – 288 с.

ISBN 978-617-7744-30-5

Є книги присвячені різним темам, наприклад, як використовувати певне програмне забезпечення, як навчитися в'язати, як управляти транспортним засобом і т.д. Мало книжок, одначе, навчають розташуванню духу для початку і закінчення будь-якої справи. Ця книга робить саме це. Якщо ви будуєте будинок, навчаєтеся або працюєте, – ви можете знайти щось корисне в цій книзі щоб завершити вашу справу.

Книга розрахована на читачів будь-якого віку.

**УДК 821.111**

ISBN 978-617-7744-30-5

# Acknowledgements

Thank God.

Thank you to my family for taking on a lot of day-to-day tasks which allowed me to complete the work.

Thank you to you, the reader, for using this book!

# Table of contents

6

7

# THANKSGIVING

## Out of many troubles

Out of many troubles God delivered me,
Out of the hand of evil people He saved me.
Let my joyful song ring,
Let my loving heart sing!

Oh God, thank You for Your glorious deeds,
For Your Love, Your call – life-giving seeds!
Tremendous is Your support!
You are the Invincible Fort!

Thank You, Lord, for everyone and everything!
Let my thankful song ring!

*Sunday – Monday*                    *17-18.02.2013*


## If I said: my foot slipped

If I said: my foot slipped,
Your mercy, o Lord, helped me.
You always helped and never skipped.
Let Your slave remember Your mercies and praise Thee!

*Thursday*                    *21.07.2016*

# Love God with all your heart

Love God with all your heart,
Neither then, nor already, but today.
He loves us unconditionally, not in part,
For what we need, let us pray!

*March*                              *2012*


# All you, people

All you, people, congregation,
Pour your heart before the Lord – our Help – at all times
As an individual, as a family and a nation.
Compose to Him sincere, joyful and grateful rhymes!

Sunday                              17.07.2016


# Glorify God in all your deeds
Glorify God in all your deeds,
Both big and small.
Let your praise precede your needs;
Open your heart and thankfully call.

Don't doubt,
As long as strength abides,
Whether in or out,
Glorify God in a quiet prayer and presentation slides!
*Sunday*                         *11.12.2011*

# Sacrifice of praise

More than a charitable donation
Is the sacrifice of praise –
The fruit of lips that is a sincere proclamation
And a quiet prayer without laze…

*Sunday*                                    *19.08.2018*


# Love God with all your heart, soul and mind

Love God with all your heart!
This will make your labour easy to start,
And other things will follow;
Your house will not be hollow.

Love God with all your soul!
You will achieve your goal,
Whether you study or work,
Whether you eat with chopsticks or fork.

Love God with all your mind!
You will not be left behind,
You will advance!
Wisdom is here, it is not given by chance.

*Sunday*                                    *21.10.2012*

# Do kind things to your neighbour

Do kind things to your neighbour,
Observe God's will this way.
You will advance in your labour
In God's blessing you'll stay!

*Saturday*                    *28.10.2012*


# Love God with all your thought

Love God with all your heart
And bravely act!
Let your love be full and not in part,
Let not routine of everyday distract.

You have so many gifts,
Believe and act!
Do honestly your shifts,
But also use wit to promptly react!

*June – July*                    *2012*


# You, o Lord, will save

They chase those whom You have wounded, who are in pain;
They are not ashamed to show disdain;
They are after those whom You have afflicted.
Oh, how much they have made their mind restricted!

They covered their ears when the poor yelped.
Let them repent and see by Whom the wounded, the afflicted,
and the poor are helped.
For if You allow tribulations to pass, they are for a time (so is
wealth),
But Your mercies and protection endure forever and it is You
Who blesses with health.

*May – June*                    *2018*


# True believers

Who are true believers?
They are the ones who stay when it is tough –
They are non-leavers –
They do not give up their friend in water that's rough.

They start a task with hope
That they can win,
That God helps to cope;
He more than just exists, He loves, He helps overcome a sin.

When they see a person in a less fortunate range,
True believers offer some help:
Be it a cup of hot coffee or some change –
They do not harden their hearts when the poor yelp.

*Monday*                    *20.02.2017*

# My refuge and my shield

God is my refuge and my shield:
I will not stumble whether I go through a dark forest or a bright
field.
He is my support and I rely on Him in all.
He is my Saviour and Father and hears my every call.

*Tuesday*                    *07.11.2017*


# Praise God with all your heart!

Praise God with all your heart!
You may be sad,
Know, though, that God loves you from the very start!
Let your kind soul be cheerfully glad!

It may be hard
Because the world is cruel;
Whole nations are eaten as lard...
Don't give up, let people see the shining of your jewel!

*Saturday*                    *17.12.2011*


# Thankful and happy

More than anything else I am thankful truly
And, therefore, happy fully.

Despite all hardships and fails
Toward the positive stuff I set my sails.

Although I may fear –
Let my courage make it disappear.
Although I may stumble –
Let God's grace make me humble.

*Tuesday*                    *20.06.2017*

# By God's Grace

I am more educated than my instructors
Because I reflect on God's ways.
I am more vigilant than orchestra conductors
Because I listen to God since the youth of my days.

He made me wiser than the old
Because I follow His commandments day and night.
He makes me whole and bold
Because I glorify Him with all my heart, knowledge, and might.

*Monday*                    *06.11.2017*

# All in all

You are my all in all!
When I hunger, You give me food;

When I thirst, You hear my call;
When I am lonely, You change to cheer my mood.

Thank Thee, Father, – You are always near!
You disperse my fear;
You make my view clear.
You make me as fast as a deer!

*Thursday*                    *21.07.2016*


# Give thanks to God with a cheerful heart

Give thanks to God with a cheerful heart –
Cheerful praise is well pleasing to Him truly.
Give thanks early in the morning from the start;
Rejoice in Him fully!

*Wednesday*                   *22.06.2016*


# Thank You, Father, for Your mighty deeds!

Thank You, Father, for Your mighty deeds!
You gave us life,
You attended to all our needs,
You gave us victory in strife.
*Wednesday*                   *22.06.2016*

# All I have I owe to God

All that I have, I owe to God:
My teeth, my eyes, my feet.
He raises me from every fall;
He nourishes me with fruit and wheat.

Peace and freedom are given by Him.
He strengthens me with a prayer!
His love and support for us never cease!
All that I have, I have by His care.

*Sunday*                              *16.11.2014*


# Do not get used to wonders

Do not get used to wonders
Because they are so many around:
Sunrises, wind, and thunders...
All is good on, above, and in the ground.

What an incredible world, look!
You'll see its majesty in all,
Listen! How sweet is the sound of a tender brook!
Also, a tiny molecule, Everest which is so tall.

These are our treasures,
Thank God! We are rich!
And these are the real pleasures,
It's all true without a hitch.
*Sunday*                              *13.04.2008*

# Thank You!

Oh God Father, thank You
For kind people around!
Thank You for the crystals of life which we call 'dew'!
Thank You for a forest creek sound!

If not Your gracious support,
I would be in the kingdom of night.
But Your Word is Life, an invincible fort!
You cure my wound, You make my burden light!

*Tuesday*                    *19.08.2011*


# When you have all

When you have all,
When your life is calm,
Remember your God
And you'll suffer no harm.

Remember those needy,
They are so poor indeed.
Please, be kind,
Deathlike is greed.

To live,
Please, open your heart –
Be happy, do good.
Much depends on your part.
*Saturday*                    *10.10.2009*

# Oh that men would praise the Lord

Praise the Lord for He is Gracious!
He takes your foot out of hardships and puts it in a place which
is spacious.
Praise the Lord and sacrifice the sacrifice of thanksgiving!
Let your praise be living!

*Sunday*                                    *03.05.2015*


# Give thanks

Give thanks to the Lord in any season –
For this, you do not need a reason,
But even if it were so, think with how much you've been
bestowed!
You've been forgiven all that you owed.

So, cheer up – you have a bright head!
You have an awesome stature.
Enough being sad, smile instead!
You love God and your neighbour,
You will certainly win with your kind nature!
You will thrive in your labour!

*Sunday*                                    *19.04.2015*

# When things are not working out

When things are not working out,
Have courage to smile;
When the time comes and you figure out,
Thank God and those who helped you cover the mile! =)

*Tuesday*                    *28.02.2017*


# For all

Father, thank Thee for all!
I have said "all" on purpose, that's true –
It's not laziness, but my soul's call.
I couldn't thank for a thing or two
'Cause it's so easy for me to forget
And all I have is not mine –
It belongs to Thee as well as my life,
But I do not regret.
Thank Thee, Father, for all!
For all Your gifts and love,
For preventing me from a fall,
For clothes and food, for the peace dove.

*Sunday*                    *06.08.2006*

# According to the abundance of the grief of my heart

According to the abundance of the grief of my heart,
O Lord, You helped me.
Your encouragements make my worries depart;
You show me the forest and make me distinguish a tree.

Your encouragements console my soul;
Your Grace fills my bowl;
You are close in distress;
You keep at bay any stress.

*Friday*                                    *22.07.2016*


# The Lord has become a place of refuge for me

The Lord has become a place of refuge for me
And my God the Helper of my hope.
With Him it is not "I" anymore, but "We";
With Him, we can cope.

*Friday*                                    *22.07.2016*

# Praise God with a grateful heart

Praise God with a grateful heart.
Let your praise, both big and small be sincere.
Have time to say "Thank You" to Him whether you go far or near.
God will make a way, continue doing your part.

*Thursday*                                    *04.08.2016*


# Oh God Almighty, make me wise

Oh God Almighty, make me wise!
Let misfortunes not surprize.
In all things let your slave serve Your Gracious Will!
Reinforce my heart to climb over the hill!

*Sunday*                                    *04.11.2012*


# The Lord is the strength of those who approach Him with fear

The Lord is the strength of those who approach Him with fear.
To them He is not far, but near.
Fear God and let Him be your Friend.
Let Him help you at the beginning and be with you at the end.

*Wednesday*                                    *08.06.2016*

# In God we shall do a might y thing

In God we shall do a mighty thing.
We will overcome the enemy completely.
To Him Who saved us we will sing.
Of His mighty deeds we will speak concretely.

*Wednesday*                    *22.06.2016*


# They have surrounded and encircled me

They have surrounded and encircled me,
But I have overcome them by the Name of the Lord completely.
They were going to advance, but had to flee.
God's work is revealed to those who believe not abstractly, but
concretely.

Lord, may Your slave be faithful,
Let Your slave be grateful.
Let Your slave speak of Your magnificent deeds.
Let Your might help your slaves in their needs.

*Sunday*                    *22.05.2016*


# Thank Thee, Heavenly Father

Thank Thee, Heavenly Father, for all:
For preventing from a fall,

For land and water, day and night,
For all Thy world which is so bright!

Thou gave me a precious gift – my life,
And Thy support is immense.
My house is rife;
In Thee I always find defence!

Thank Thee for loving hearts around.
How reviving is their sound!
Thank Thee for food –
For both, body and soul, it is good.

I know, just words are not sufficient,
But help to my neighbour, good deeds!
And Thou will make us proficient
And send all or even more a human being needs!

*Tuesday – Saturday*                     *13-17.11.2007*


# Thank God for all!

Thank God for all!
When I cry to You, You hear my call.
Out of many troubles You have delivered Your free-will slave
And whenever I fall, You raise me up, shake off the dust, and save.

You blessed me with success in all things.
When I feel low, You spread my wings.
Wherever I go, You are there:
Here on earth, far in space – You are close, You care.
*Sunday*                     *13.02.2016*

41

# Declare God's works

God has delivered you out of a deep pit;
Out of many troubles He saved.
Declare God's works with rejoicing,

And let your words be seasoned with wit!
With good deeds let your words be paved.
Let your praise be with a cheerful voicing!

*Sunday*                                    *30.05.2015*


# Thank God

Thank God in simplicity of heart,
Not because you have to,
But because you have a plentiful cart,
Because you love and the love is true.

*2014-2015*


# For all I've got

For all I've got
I am obliged to Thee:
For the loving family and abundant pot,
For the grass and for the tree.

I sinned a lot,
But Thou art Gracious,
Thou can cure even a sot,
Thou can make him vivacious.

Father, please,
Forgive and save us all,
Thy Grace is sweeter than honey of bees,
We turn to Thee, don't let us fall.

*Friday*                              *25.11.2005*

# Give thanks to the Lord for He is Good

Give thanks to the Lord for He is Good,
His mercy endures forever!
He provides us with water and food;
He makes us strong and clever.

*Sunday*                              *26.07.2015*

# Bless the Lord, all you His servants

Bless the Lord, all you His servants
Bless the Lord, all you who come to Church,
Who spend your time in constant search
Of His Love and Way!
Bless the Lord when you do, when you speak, when you pray!
*Tuesday*                    *14.07.2015*

# Make me hear Your lovingkindness in the morning

Make me hear Your lovingkindness in the morning
For I trust in You each day.
Make me know the way I should go in life and learning
For I lift up my soul to You and pray.

*Sunday*                    *01.08.2015*

# Praise the Lord

Praise the Lord in any situation;
Praise the Lord among any nation;
Praise God in word, in deed, in thought,
Just as Jesus Christ taught.

Let your praise be with cheer!
Do kind things, say kind words without fear.
Have salt in yourself and have taste.
Be smart, go beyond copy and paste.

Be clever in things big and small.
Praise the Lord in all!

*Sunday*                    *26.04.2015*

# LOVE

## Exceedingly great love

When a worry sneaks in,
Do not give in,
Hold your ground:
You will enjoy victorious sound

Because God loved you
With love that is exceedingly great:
Wherever you go, it is attached as if with glue.
It is a blessing to realize it early rather than late.

*Sunday*                                    *10.03.2019*


## Alone

Never be alone
Unless you need to.
God created woman from man's bone
And bode her to help him break through.

Saint Paul instructs to love your wife
As Christ loved the Church – in the truth, forgiveness, care.
Beautify with love and good deeds your life;
Discover, awesomize, dare.

*Thursday*                                    *30.08.2018*

# God loves us much more than we realize

God loves us much more than we realize.
Remember? Believe!
Smile, be bold, awesomize;
Let sadness not prevail, build, shine, live.

*Friday*                                    *22.02.2019*

# Positive

Be patient, forgive each other;
Gird yourselves with love for God and your brother;
Let God's peace prevail in you
For you are called to it, it's true.

Be grateful, teach and perfect in wisdom each day,
Whether at work or at play.
Let your faith and love be seen in acts;
Let your words be based on the truth and your judgement – on
facts.

*Wednesday*                                    *13.02.2019*

# Speak to me when I rejoice

Speak to me when I rejoice
To make my happiness full at the sound of your voice!

Speak to me when I am sad
To help me overcome the things which are bad!

Because your love is true,
Because your tears are dew,
Because your eyes are blue,
Because I love you!

*Sunday – Monday*                    *26-27.08.2012*


# Much more

God loves us much more than we can imagine indeed:
He fights for us, He cares, He feeds, He helps in every need.
Therefore, despair is a big sin;
However hard – be smart, repair, win.

*Sunday*                    *10.02.2019*


# How to be united

Being united is good,
But how to unite?
Around culture, interests, food?
Temporary sunset and sunrise or the True Light?

Christ is the True Light,
But realization of this should come from inside.

Cultivate what the Bible teaches with all your might;
Invite others to join this ride.

*Sunday*                                     *06.01.2019*

# A family and a nation must be united

A family and a nation must be united –
That way, their journey will be lighted,
Their obstacles will be overcome;
To their enemies, they will be able to say, "Come, get some!"

In all, however, they must praise God with hearts sincere –
They will go far, they won't go near;
They will achieve what they want and more;
They will get all they need and will keep some goods in store.

*Sunday*                                     *06.01.2019*

# Care for each other

You're brothers indeed,
So, care for each other.
To have a good crop, you need a good seed,
So, care for each other.

When you can, do,
Help your suffering brother.

He is so tired, it's true,
Help your suffering brother.

All your deeds are noted down,
No doubt, you will be paid back.
Listen to your kind heart sound,
No doubt you will be paid back!

*Sunday*                                    *09.03.2008*


# To my friend

My religious friend,
You've been my consolation
When the world seemed to have approached the end, –
'God', you said, 'is our Salvation'.

Thank you, my friend.
Your love is pure gold,
Your advice lends a hand,
Your word warms when it's cold!

When I was in need of understanding,
When I got tired of the lack of love around,
You reminded where we were standing –
That Christ's doctrine is still and always sound.

*Saturday*                                  *18.02.2012*

# Two commandments

Love God with all your mind, might and heart;
Let love be full and not in part.
Love your neighbour and thyself alike.
Each day let love bring in some light!

*Sunday*                                    *04.09.2011*


# Let love inside

Let love inside,
In your mind and heart.
It will provide
You with good things from the start.

Let love inside,
Let it shine to your neighbour!
Let your mind be wide;
Let love make easy your labour.

*Wednesday – Thursday     13-14.10.2010*


# If love is being happy about little things

If love is being happy about little things,
I want to be there, letting go stings.
If love means forgiving sincerely,
I want to do this fully, not merely.

If love means getting rid of fears,
I want this to happen and to wipe off your tears.
If love means to share good things,
I want you to be close for all that life brings.

*Monday*                    *06.03.2017*


# Love love and it will cling to you

Love love and it will cling to you.
Love God, neighbour; and yourself in a smart way though.
This requires dedication, true.
Be big on gentleness, on grumpiness be low.

Do your exercises, eat veggies, rest;
Hit the books and work with zest.
Say "thank you" for all good things.
Enjoy each moment that life brings.

*2018*


# Love love and seek it

Love love and do what's in your power
To be sweet & salty and not sour.
Love love and always seek it –
To preserve this gift use your heart and wit.

*Thursday*                    *14.06.2018*

# Mothers

Most mothers, I believe,
Qualify for sainthood truly.
They love, they sacrifice, they forgive;
They are not afraid of the unruliest bully.

*Sunday*                                      *15.04.2018*


# New commandment

We have received a new commandment truly:
"Love each other".
This is how they will know that we are Christians fully:
When we treat people as a sister and a brother.

*Wednesday*                                   *18.04.2018*


# Fragile planet
Take care, friend,
Take care of nature before it's too late at the end.
Nature is tender, vulnerable, and fragile.
Will it stand suffering forever or for a short while?

Take care, friend,
Of the world around, whatever the modern trend.
Start with yourself today:
While the sun shines make your hay.
*Sunday*                                      *11.12.2011*

# When we get married, girl

When we get married, girl,
The heavens will rejoice.
Together we will be looking for the Pearl.
People will be happy about our choice.

*Monday*                    *20.02.2017*


# Love your neighbour as you love yourself

Have you ever thought
That loving others
As we love ourselves, which should be a lot,
Is being accepting of your sisters and brothers?

It is being forgiving and patient in all;
Loving God, including in His creation;
Being happy, faithful, hopeful, and tall
Despite shortcomings and an awkward business presentation?

Love God and love your neighbour,
Love yourself in studies, rest, and labour.
Smile often whenever you can.
Melting ice inside and keeping positive is the plan!

*Friday – Sunday*                    *02-04.02.2018*

# When you are in need of love and care

When you are in need of love and care,
There is Someone out there:
Whether you stand or fall, Christ is with you.
He more than just exists – He loves and cares to get you
through.

Continue rowing knowing this.
You will achieve more than you miss.
Do not get desperate whatsoever.
Smile, get ready to win, be clever!

*Sunday*                                        *30.04.2017*


# Hey, what are you doing for the rest of your life?

When you meet the one, the husband or the wife,
It's more than just "how is your day",
It's "hey, what are you doing for the rest of your life?"
"We'll share all things, we'll dance, we'll sing, we'll pray".

When this happens, be sincere;
Be able to keep silence, say a smart joke;
Be not away on your phone, be with him/her here.
When the time comes, share whatever yoke.

*Saturday – Tuesday*                    *13-16.05.2017*

# Smart & steady

You can be my smart and fun,
And I can be your strong and steady.
We can help each other to run,
To get things faster ready!

*Monday*                    *20.02.2017*


# You make me feel right

You make me feel right.
Even in a situation that's tight,
Your smile, your word of support
Are my place of refuge, my protective fort.

*Sunday*                    *19.02.2017*


# Don't be afraid of saying good, kind words

Don't be afraid of speaking about your feelings in life;
Don't be afraid of saying good, kind words however harsh is the daily strife.
Be bold to say the words "I love you!",
And they will follow you as if attached with super glue.

*Sunday*                    *28.01.2018*

# God loves us

God loves us – we know.
But the thing is we have to live it –
Whether we fly high or fall low.
Let's act with faith and wit!

*Sunday*                                    *10.12.2017*


# Superstitions

Beware of superstitions in life and labour:
They prevent from achieving personal goals.
They are in the way of loving God and helping your neighbour;
When you are cold – they are ice, when you are hot – they are
burning coals.

*Thursday*                                  *30.11.2017*


# Love is all I have, it's true

Love is all I have, it's true.
Love is what helps me break through.
But what else does a person need,
Whatever is her or his honest breed?

Life is different for a loving heart,
Simple happiness is its part.

Spread shoulders and bright eyes...
Love is a dove that flies!

*Thursday*                    *04.12.2008*


# Wisdom and love

Proceed with wisdom and love in all,
Whether you are gaining a score or losing the ball.
In all good things use those
To come on time, to get a degree, to surprise your sweetheart
with a rose.

*Sunday*                    *17.10.2017*


# Respect your woman

Respect your woman, gent.
Put her before play, work, rent.
Not only will she be your blessing day and night,
You yourself will feel confident, light!

*Tuesday*                    *17.10.2017*

# Hey, girl

Hey, girl, what are you doing
For the rest of your life?
We can share things, sing, go canoeing.
Do you want to become my wife?

*Tuesday*                    *17.10.2017*


# Love as if tomorrow never comes

Love as if tomorrow never comes
Despite the unknown that numbs.
Love as if you had only one day;
Love for your life happens today.

*Sunday*                    *29.10.2017*


# It's never too late

It's never too late,
Whatever you feel.
Go ahead, what for to wait?
Rust covers resting steel.

When everything seems to be lost,
Start from the beginning.
Still there is something which is beyond any cost…
The bell of life inside of you is ringing!

It's never too late,
Just try!
What else to state?
Believe, wisdom makes people fly!

*Saturday*                    *22.03.2008*


# The key to the Kingdom

Love is the key
To the Kingdom of God truly.
It sets you free,
It makes you grow fully.

Love disperses fear;
Love wipes off every tear.
It cures hurt,
It builds rapport.

Love your neighbour,
Let it be small, but sincere.
Let your way be known far and near,
May both of you succeed in your labour.

If you want to enter the Kingdom ever,
Have love in stock;
In your kind deeds, be clever;
Love the Pastor and love the flock.

*Monday*                    *09.10.2017*

# All you do, do this with love

All you do, do this with love:
Studying, working, returning a glove.
Let love help you decide
And right answers provide.

*Sunday*                    *08.09.2013*


# With love

Whatever you do,
Let it be with love and faith truly,
Add hope to get through –
Live your life fully.

*Saturday*                    *26.08.2017*


# Whatever happens, stick together

Whatever happens, stick together,
In a bad storm and in good weather,
To overcome all misfortunes;
You will feel like a feather.

Supposing, you fall – you'll get a support,
Each of you will stand like a fort!
He, who'll try to defeat you, will lose.
You'll be like a glorious caravel which enters a port.

Whatever you plan, you will do
'Cause on God your hopes will be fixed by both of you.
Love is your shield,
You are protected from burning arrows, it's true.

Beauty decays, love never ends.
Rudeness destroys, a kind word mends.
Stick together, good friends!

*Tuesday – Friday*          *19-22.02.2008*


# Love God (1)

Love God in trouble and joy!
All your mind, all your strength, and all your heart you will need
to employ.
Be afraid of no one
But Him, be ready to wait, be ready to run.

Love God with all your strength,
With all your mind, heart, and body length!
Let your heart not sink:
He will support you more than you think.

Rely on Him and go.
Let your kindness grow!
Be quick and smart;
In studies, in work, strengthen your heart!

Be afraid of no one, not anybody in sum.
Only fear God now and in the time to come –

You will bring abundant fruit,
You will grow a profound root!

*Saturday – Sunday*                    *19-20.01.2013*


# When I close my eyes

When I close my eyes,
I see you, baby.
I won't tell lies.
Am I crazy? Maybe.

I don't wonna lose you.
Hearing everywhere your voice:
In a gentle wind, in a kitten's mew;
You are my choice.

Even if I go away,
I will miss you again.
If I am not able to stay,
I will always miss you then…

*Saturday – Sunday*                    *26-27.01.2008*


# Have you ever seen a sunrise

Have you ever seen a sunrise
Or the azure above

Which is often called just skies?
Have you ever been in love?

Or haven't you got time enough?
Vanity of vanities, too much of it
And the sea of life is so rough.
Bustle can so badly hit...

But I don't say forget all, throw away.
Just let love inside, right into your heart.
Mind your way.

*Saturday*                    *16.09.2006*


# Forgive me if you have ever forgiven

Forgive me if you have ever forgiven,
I'm going to strive as I have never striven.
I know that it was my mistake.
Don't let your feelings drown in your heart's lake.

Baby, just tell me what I shall do,
I cannot imagine my future without you.
Do you really want to break up with me?
Forgive me as you always forgave me.

*Saturday*                    *21.05.2010*

# Love (1)

Love is a distant star.
When we are going close or far,
It helps us find the way.
Have love in yourself and pray!

*Saturday*                              *18.04.2015*


## Love (2)

Love.
What else?
Like a white dove…
It cures, brings good health.
Real love is a shield for the soul.
In summer it is like a gulp of fresh juice,
In winter it is better than coal.
Love is rich & that's the truth;
Love is young and mature,
It will win in any strife.
With love we endure.
Love is life!

*Sunday*                              *03.02.2008*


# Marriage

Marriage is a mystery indeed.
Treat it as such:

Help your spouse who is in need
Of love, support, and care so much!

*Tuesday*                    *28.02.2017*


# She's a pretty girl

She's a pretty girl,
And he's a handsome guy
Nothing can be compared to her, even a pearl,
But he's risking to lose her if he doesn't try.

Everybody will say that he'll then regret…
Hey, don't let your love pass by!
Sincerity will always be normally met.
Nothing bad will happen if you try.

*Saturday*                    *19.02.2005*


# You walk about the world

You walk about the world
With your eyes open and hair curled,
Now happier, now sadder
Just climbing little by little the ladder.

Sometimes you stumble and fly into temper.
But what's the use? Doesn't it hamper?

There is a remedy for all, not new:
Be strong to say 'I love you'.

*Saturday*                                    *27.05.2006*


# Alberta

I am Alberta-bound.
I fell in love with this province completely;
In no other place have I found
Air which blows so sweetly;

Mountains which soar so acutely;
Lakes with water so fresh and lots of fish;
Deer, squirrels, bunnies that run freely absolutely.
Alberta, wherever I travel, you are my wish.

*Saturday*                                    *11.07.2015*


# I saw you in a bus

I saw you in a bus,
How pretty you were!
Another day of city fuss…
Both alone among those people in fur.

With bright, shining eyes you were standing;
It was cold outside.

In your eyes I saw understanding;
The world for me became wide.

*Wednesday – Sunday*                    *23-27.01.2008*


# I still love you

I love you like crazy –
Although sometimes lazy –
I want to give you all:
Flowers, kisses, support, joy big and small!

*Saturday*                              *28.01.2017*


# Everyone needs to be needed

Everyone needs to be needed
And one more thing in addition –
In your heart you will read it:
"You need to help with no recognition".

*Tuesday*                               *05.05.2009*


# I like the sound of your name

I like when you are around –
It's like serotonin and vitamin D that abound.

Your eyes are of the most beautiful hue;
I like speaking with you.

You make hard things light:
Your ideas are effortless, bright.
I am your gent, you are my dame;
I like the sound of your name.

*Thursday*                    *12.01.2017*


# Your friend is not worse

Your friend is not worse,
Just different perhaps.
No one puts the cart before the horse.
Try to love her/him without giving slaps.

*Thursday*                    *12.01.2017*


# Life is momentarily, true

Life is momentarily, true,
Your family is always with you.
How important it is to feel their support!
When you are happy or sad, they're your Fort!

*Thursday*                    *31.12.2009*

# You are so beautiful without knowing this

You are so beautiful without knowing this.
I like the way you look,
Your heart, your kiss.
You are my friend, more than my favourite book.

*Monday*                    *26.12.2016*


# Pretty girl, don't cry

Pretty girl, don't cry;
He left you, but try.
Wipe off your tears and fly
On the wings of your dreams so high.

You left her, what for
Still seeking anything more?
You say you broke no law –
I say you declared a war.

What a disaster a hypocrite heart can bring –
It's like a sharp sting
Which hurts a bird's wing
Not allowing her to fly or to sing.

*Saturday*                    *03.12.2005*

# Smile, I love your smile

(Dedicated to Ryley and Joele)

Smile, I love your smile.
You are so beautiful when you do!
I love your own amazing style.
Your smile helps get through =)

*Monday*                    *12.12.2016*


# In love

Baby, I am in love with your hair,
Your voice, your gaze, your smile;
Your looks are fair;
I love your style.

I want to share all things with you.
You are the only one for me;
Your faith, your hope, your love are true;
With you I want to raise a family.

*Sunday*                    *25.09.2016*


# Years pass fast

One hundred years pass faster than you think –
Like a click on a website link –

Say that kind word, do that kind deed,
Plant a good seed.

*Sunday*                                    *22.10.2016*


# Forgive

Forgive although you were right.
Forgive to make your heart light.
Forgive not because of what they do,
But because of who you are, because God loves you.

*Friday*                                    *14.10.2016*


# Live. Laugh. Love

Live as if you had only one day.
Laugh as if you were a child at play.
Love as if that's all you've got to say.

*Sunday*                                    *09.10.2016*


# Sincere smile

Sincere smile, how much it means!
It is like bread and oil, beans

For a hungry soul.
For a fan it is a goal.

Just smile and improve the world around.
The birds are singing, what a sound!
The past is past, we live in the present.
Your smiling face is so pleasant!

Your smile is a cure for others,
It does support your brothers.
Be yourself, it is worthwhile.
How much it means, sincere smile!

*Friday*                              *12.12.2008*

# Happy birthday, baby girl

Happy birthday to you,
You are my baby girl!
I am happy to have found you.
You are my precious pearl!

*Sunday*                              *25.09.2016*

# We all need attention

We all need attention –
Not only you and me, but our neighbour too.

To concentrate on ourselves is a temptation,
But communication cures, it's true.

*Monday – Tuesday*                    *04-05.06.2007*


# When you meet a special someone

When you meet a special someone
And it doesn't work the way you want at once,
Don't worry – your thing will not be gone.
Stock up with patience for a year, a day or a month.

*Sunday*                              *14.08.2016*


# To forgive

When I do wrong, I ask to forgive.
The Father and people always do and so I happily live.
But how often, how easy do I pardon in turn?
I have so much to learn…

I am aching for a change,
I believe I am able to arrange.
I only pray for being sage,
I do need wisdom which never knows rage.

But first of all I want to thank.
People are kind to me who has neither much money nor a high
rank.

Thank Thee, Father, for all,
Especially for love, Thou hear every call!

*Sunday*                        *15.07.2007*


# Wise men keep silence

Wise men keep silence
When love speaks.
No words, no violence.
Even birds watch their beaks.

Love is calm,
But is loud as well.
It makes its nest on a farm,
But also where no one is able to dwell.

Whatever good one can think,
It can be about love.
Love is the strongest link,
Wise men know this as well as a dove.

*Saturday*                        *06.05.2006*


# More important than money
♥ ♥ ♥

More important than money,
More important than food.

Better than honey,
Lighter than wood.

It is weak…
But stronger than rock.
It is a clear creek.
Wider than ocean, faster than clock.

Above all it is kind,
Jealousy melts like coal.
It brings to Heaven a devoted mind.
It heals a soul.

*Monday*                    *14.12.2009*


# Mother

More than just a kind heart…
One remark and a thousand smiles.
This is love and not in part.
Here is what helps to cover miles.
Either end of this poem is true,
Right is the beginning and the full stop is too.

*Sunday*                    *21.05.2006*

# Tea for two

Tea for two and two for tea –
Good reason to meet for you and for me,
To speak about our day
And to exchange glances that speak more than words can say.

*Bright Monday*          *02.05.2016*

# Live your life as if tomorrow would never come

Live your life as if tomorrow would never come:
Do good, be aware of harm;
Make peace with all and those you love,
For your enemy – pick up his glove.

For we never know
If the number of our years will be high or low.
So, let's be prepared today –
Let your kindness show up without delay…

*Sunday*                    *06.11.2011*

# When love comes, it's so quiet

When love comes, it's so quiet –
No struggle, no riot.

But real love soon becomes loud
Muffing every other sound.

Love is calm, but strong,
Love is never wrong;
It keeps silent, but speaks much,
Love is like a rose petal touch.

Love tells the truth.
It never vanishes, it's stable and smooth.
Love melts anger and is smart,
Keep open your heart.

*Sunday*                    *18.12.2005*


# Canadian girls

Canadian girls are gentle and brave;
They like hockey, music, and know how to save;
They are intelligent and amazing
In winter frost, and in the sun which is blazing.

*Monday*                    *29.02.2016*


# When we speak about love which is true

When we speak about love which is true,
We should also mention respect all the way through.
Suffering and sacrifice can mingle too,

But also a lot of happiness and – in terms of mood – more pink than blue.

*Wednesday*                                  *10.02.2016*

# Love God with a sincere heart

Be happy and love God with a sincere heart,
He is your Friend Who will never depart.
Love also your neighbour, friend,
Be truthful, let your sober account on him never depend.

Love yourself in a smart way:
Not to stuck more chocolate in your face,
But to improve your body and soul,
To make with God's help your life truly whole!

*August*                                     *2014*

# You are the only thing that's blinding

The sun is shining,
But you are the only thing that's blinding.
All this time, girl, where have you been hiding?
You are like a yacht that's gliding.

We enjoy our shared time
You write the best greetings for me, and I compose you a rhyme.

We cook and enjoy our meal together.
When we pray we are lighter than a feather.

*Sunday*                              *10.01.2016*


# 1 Corinthians 13

Have you ever asked what love is?
Check 1 Corinthians 13, please.
What do you think?
Would you share it via a link?

*Saturday*                            *28.11.2015*


# If I had never met you

What would I do
If I had never met you?
I could be a better blogger then;
I might draw the world map with my pen.

I could go to a pub every night.
But, girl, I wouldn't trade all that and more for going with you
to fly a kite,
For kissing you, babe, and listening to you speaking about your
day,
For our marriage and the chance to jointly pray.

*Thursday*                            *19.11.2015*

# Like a lady

Treat your woman like a lady all the time
And when you fall, she'll help you climb.
She deserves to be treated like a princess, man.
She deserves that you should become her devoted fan.

*Thursday*                    *19.11.2015*


# Girlfriend and boyfriend

Always treat your girlfriend like a lady;
Remember to tell her "baby".
Make sure that when she is with you,
She has the support to lean on like a faithful captain and his
crew.

Treat your boyfriend like a gentleman
Regardless of how many things he can.
Just have respect and understanding and he'll reward you too:
He will be your support and stimulus to get through.

*Friday*                    *13.11.2015*


# She's got a cross around her neck

She's got a cross around her neck.
She's good at modern tech.

Her hair is like a toy,
I enjoy it like a boy.

Her eyes are wealth of love,
They raise me up and make me fly above.
I like her voice which is delighted,
It makes me feel excited.

*Saturday*                    *07.11.2015*


# Let us carry love into the open air

Whatever happens around,
Let us be prepared to carry the love we share
Into the open air.
Only by sharing love we can make it abound.

*Saturday*                    *31.10.2015*


# She thinks I'm a superman

She thinks I am a superman
Because I've got a PhD,
But it's not about the degree,
Not about things I can.

It's all about her:
She has a loving heart,

The sense of wonder from the start.
She is not after gold or fur,

She is after me.
It's not about a degree,
It is about us.
It is about my super baby thus.

*Sunday*                              *25.10.2015*


# It's a beautiful day

It's a beautiful day
And a beautiful girl;
I want to thankfully pray
She's my precious pearl.

*Saturday*                            *17.10.2015*


# As arrows in the hand of a skillful man

As arrows in the hand of a skillful man,
So are children, ensure to love them.
Loving is the plan.
In their upbringing, choose love, respect, and Orthodox
Christian stem.

*Sunday*                              *28.06.2015*

# Family

A good wife is a gift.
When it comes to work she is swift;
She is gentle and smart,
During hard times she does not depart.

A good husband is a support –
He is wise, gentle, and strong as a fort.
He comes from work as soon as he can;
To embrace his wife and his kids is the plan.

A good family is built on love and support –
They share joy, solve issues, go together for a walk and do sport.
They are a team:
They love, they build, they gleam!

*Wednesday*                                    *09.09.2015*


# In the circle of friends

Love God with all your heart,
With all your strength!
Stand firm, do not depart,
Be consistent on the way throughout its length.

If somebody goes astray
Or if you are in the circle of friends:
Keep the light of faith on your way,
Remember where all ends.
*Saturday*                                    *23.08.2014*

# The way you look tonight

You have been beautiful a million times,
But nothing can fully describe how you look tonight, not a
hundred thousand rhymes.
Something in your attentive eyes
Remind how much luckier I am than all those other guys.

Something in the way you smile,
Something in the dress and make-up style;
Something in the way you step which is so light –
You look so good tonight!

*Saturday*                                   *08.08.2015*


# How good and how pleasant it is for brothers to be together in unity

How good and how pleasant it is for brothers to be together in
unity,
How much strength it adds to the whole community.
Things get done better,
Opportunities are open faster.

When a brother relies on his brother,
They both will go farther;
Their business will succeed
When with mutual love they proceed.

*July*                                   *2015*

# My mother

I thank you, Mom, for your love so strong!
Thank you for your care.
You helped me whether I was right or wrong,
You protected me in winter frost and summer glare.

You cook best food in the world;
You covered me with a blanket when I slept curled.
When I was ill, you were with me;
When I was sad, you made my mind free.

Thank you because you are still close by.
You give advice,
You share your rice.
You just help, you never ask why.

*Saturday*                         *08.08.2015*


# Friendship, family, duty, and love

First do important things
And other things will follow.
This will help spread your wings,
Your house will not be hollow.

Wrap up important ends;
And live with love.
Remember your duty and friends
And you will earn a peace dove.
*Thursday*                         *02.06.2011*

# When I forget to be kind

When I forget to be kind,
Kind things forget me too.
A heart dies when it is blind.
Let love remain with you.

Love fills in our life.
Love – so much in the word!
To carry on in any strife…
Love saves the world.

*Saturday*                    *30.10.2010*


# Lord, You are the Same

Oh Lord, You are the Same.
You are still with us, You still cure;
You can still heal a person who is lame.
When we travel, You make our way secure.

Oh Lord, You are the Same.
Your Love is so Pure, so Deep.
You help us achieve any good aim.
You still care for Your sheep.

How great Your deeds are in our lives!
You help us cope with all.
You are beside, however deep man dives.
Oh Lord, save us all, rich and poor, big and small.

When I pray, I know You hear my prayer
Because You are the Same.
You are with us, with a jobless and a mayor.
You hear all who call upon Your Name.

*Saturday*                    *11.07.2015*


# Blessed is everyone who fears the Lord in his and her heart

Blessed is everyone who fears the Lord in his and her heart,
Who walks in His way in full, not in part.
Their children will be like olive plants around table.
If both husband and wife fear God, their marriage will be stable.

*Tuesday*                    *30.06.2015*


# Live your faith

Live your faith through deeds –
Plant kind things, avoid weeds;
Water the seed of love in your heart;
Love God, love your neighbour, love life and be smart!

*Tuesday*                    *19.05.2015*

# Love is a distant star

Love is a distant star:
It guides us home wherever we are.
Start doing things with love truly –
May God help you live fully!

*Tuesday*                    *31.03.2015*


# Love God (2)

Love God on all your ways
For you don't know the length of your days.
Do not put it off till tomorrow.
There aren't too many things to follow:

Love God with all your mind, strength, and heart.
And love your neighbour as yourself, it's not a complex art.
Your heart will prompt where to start.
Keep your shoulders straight, your head is so smart!

*Thursday*                    *11.09.2014*


# Love love

Love love and seek it at home, at work, and everywhere,
And it will yield its fruit you won't know where.
It will cling to you
As if you were covered with glue!

Love love and you will find!
If someone does not understand, never mind;
Smile and keep your way ahead.
May God's love protect you from your feet to the head!

*Saturday*                          *30.08.2014*

# HAPPINESS

## Not to take away our time

God gave us the Church and all other good things
Not to take away our time
And not because He needs anything from us or our kings,
But because He wants to help us climb.

Therefore, when we skip Church prayer,
We deprive ourselves of protection;
We push aside a crown from our own hair;
We reject God's care.

*Sunday*                              *24.03.2019*

## Share your smile

Share your smile to brighten somebody's day,
To lighten your own way,
To support when people go or stay,
To communicate more light than when you just say!

*Sunday*                              *17.03.2019*

# Prayer is a strong thing

Prayer is a strong thing.
For our body we need water and food, for our soul – prayer and good deed.
Prayer plus fasting equals a wing and a wing
Which carry us up, closer to God, indeed.

Stock up with prayer if you intend to lead
Your family, workers or a people as a king;
Start with a prayer to succeed.
Let prayer heal an offence, a wound and a sting.

Let prayer help you in every need.
God hears you whenever you pray.
When your soul is hungry, you have food to feed.
Let prayer help every day and in every good deed.

*Saturday*                    *21.02.2015*


# To be happy

To be happy we need two things:
To love and to be loved truly.
This is what helps us spread our wings
And to live fully.

God has loved us with love so strong,
Therefore, we have one part of the equation come along.
Another one, – that is to love, – is our assignment,

91

But loving God in return may be an excellent start and a perfect alignment.

*Friday*                              *01.02.2019*


# Your time will come

Your time will come
Because you can endure.
Your time will come,
Your heart is pure.

*Sunday*                              *01.02.2009*


# Grace and love

Once I got ill.
God showed grace and love then too.
I let the children in the line go first and sat still;
I did not feel worse, true.

When it was time to pay,
It turned out I had no cash.
The receptionist agreed to wait a day.
So, I called a taxi – it came in a flash.

I asked to lend me money –
The driver agreed

With an expression in heart so sunny,
Leaving no place for greed.

Thank You, Father, for all these kind deeds
And for saying to ask to be given!
You look after all our needs.
Let us remember Your words wherever we may be driven.

*Sunday*                              *24.09.2017*


# When we miss

When we miss,
We tend to lose our peace
And think about what is gone
Rather than how much hurt it could have done.

Take a bus, for example, –
And such things are ample –
What if "your" bus were to crash
And you were in such a rush.

What if the bus you did take
Can bring you faster without putting anything at stake?
What if you can serve your neighbour
And still be in time for your labour?

Therefore, try not to get upset
When things do not work out
The way you've set –
Your Father knows and cares without any doubt.
*Thursday*                          *17.01.2019*

# Just for today

Just for today,
I will be happy truly;
I will live a worry-free day;
I will fulfill my duties duly.

I will not overwork,
But I will do just right;
I will pray before I use my fork,
And I will focus on light.

*Tuesday*                    *11.12.2018*


# What you've got

If only I had… add your own.
Instead of rejoicing we moan…
Think and thank God for all you've got.
Out of that build because that is a lot.

*Sunday*                    *11.11.2018*


# Prescription

If your worries pour as biscuits from an overthrown open tin,
Or if you are in low spirits or sad –
Here is something to help you to win,
Regardless of how many sticky moments you've had.

This is a prescription,
But for it to take effect,
You have to follow it with a conviction:
One good deed a day, no need to perfect.

*Tuesday*                    *27.11.2018*


# Our bodies are like ships

Our bodies are like ships on the ocean that rages;
We are like captains who are courageous.
Our task is to direct our feet
To the safe harbour – the Kingdom of God, our fleet.

*Sunday*                    *26.08.2018*


# Diary

If you are unhappy, hey,
Start a diary with all good things
You are thankful for each day –
Big and small – all that blew air into you wings.

*Wednesday*                    *04.07.2018*

# Best bargain

The Church is the best bargain in town:
You get the most for your time;
Your spirits go up, – your trouble – down.
Come and get help in your climb.

*Wednesday*                    *18.07.2018*


# Humour

Humour is a friend,
Share with it your worries.
Use it to build and amend;
To listen to and to tell stories.

*Wednesday*                    *18.07.2018*


# A saint who is sad

A saint who is sad
Gives a reason to people to think something bad.
Therefore, rejoice as much as you can
In prayer, studies, work – in all with and without a plan.

*Sunday*                    *15.07.2018*

# However hard, rejoice

However hard, rejoice.
However slow, fast or sloppy,
Let joy be heard in your voice.
Walk, run and pet cheerfully your dog whose ears are floppy!

*Thursday*                    *31.05.2018*


# Smile and let the world smile too!

Smile and let the world smile too!
Smile, believe you can come through!
Rely on God and go.
While the sun shines – mow.

Smile, let the world smile too!
Smile, for you can win, it's true.
Your prayers are heard.
Let us rely on our Father's Word!

*Sunday – Thursday*                    *15-19.07.2012*


# Let's not be sorry

Let's not be sorry
About what we don't have now,
But let's be thankful without worry
For what we have without a row.

97

And then, in prayer, by working hard,
We may acquire more;
We may learn our hearts and souls to guard.
In the meanwhile, let's have love in store!

*Monday*                              *16.01.2012*


# **Happy because alive**

Happy because alive;
Snappy because I strive;
Thankful – I have so much;
Hopeful; with friends in touch.

Always, always, and always
I must be grateful –
As the real faithful,
All days, all days, and all days.

I don't know what is ahead.
I don't feel lack of bread.
My brain, my way, my strife.
My heart, my soul, my life.

*Sunday*                              *25.05.2008*

# Every breath is a gift

Every breath is a gift,
Rejoice, do kind, silly things, be swift.
Let your gratitude be obvious in your deeds and voice.
Whether you are going close or far, rejoice.

*Sunday*                                    *13.05.2018*


# When your hand can give, let it give

When your hand can give, let it give.
When you can save your little brother, let him live.

Our time is short,
Neither tomorrow nor later it can be caught,

Do not say 'tomorrow', 'later' or 'soon'.
Life is now, at this moment, slipping away like a balloon.

Live now, be free;
You are a blossoming tree!

Live and do good till you can,
No one will stop you or ban!

Your strength is inside.
Believe! Your kind deeds will abide…

*Wednesday*                                 *17.12.2008*

# Both hardships and treasure will fade away

Both hardships and treasure will fade away,
But love is forever.
Watch what you do, what you say,
Decide for yourself what is clever.

There are things, deeds, and words that lead to death.
Faith, hope, love are the way of life.
Believe till the last breath.
To mow peace, do not plant or engage in strife.

*Saturday*                    *09.06.2007*


# Never be sorry that you have missed

Never be sorry that you have missed
An incredible chance,
That you haven't been kissed,
That you have failed in a dance.

Keep doing good, kind things;
Have courage in stock;
Welcome the grace that the present moment brings.
Thank God for both an open and a closed lock.

*Saturday*                    *17.06.2017*

# In any situation

In any situation
Remain your kind self ever –
In joy and frustration –
Be simple, joyful, and clever!

*Wednesday*                    *21.03.2018*


# Be happy (1)

Be happy – however hard it is;
Spend time with your family however busy you are.
Enjoy honey although it comes with bees.
Rejoice in God whether you are going close or far.

*Saturday*                    *10.02.2018*


# When you are in doubt – pray

When you are in doubt – pray
In the morning, at night, during the day;
Whether long or short, let the prayer come from the heart.
Let it be with faith, hope, love fully, not in part.

*Thursday*                    *10.08.2017*

# Sometimes you lose

Sometimes you lose,
But sometimes you find.
I see that you snooze,
Wake up, it isn't time to be blind!

Instead of mourning
Over what you don't possess,
Listen carefully to this warning,
Be glad at what you have, be glad at less.

*Sunday*                                    *16.01.2005*


# Rejoice (1)

Rejoice, do not be sad,
You are alive and can achieve so much!
What else to be said?
Be glad for you are a Christian and should be as such.

Be happy and let not your hands go down –
God is with you;
He is Strong to put on you a PhD gown –
Rejoice, God's love is your support everywhere and always, it's
true.

Not only this, but you love Him truly.
He, be sure, sees this
And will reward you duly.
Rejoice to hit the target and not to miss.
*Saturday*                          *19.08.2017*

# Rejoice in life and live!

Rejoice in life and live!
Praise God and thankful be.
You have so much, believe.
Here is an example: an ant and a bee.

They work with an easy heart,
They are glad they are alive
And are happy about every body part.
Don't worry, one day all flowers thrive.

You are more than that!
You are man!
God will make your road smooth and flat.
Rejoice, enjoy your fruit and bread with bran!

*Sunday*                                    *25.07.2017*


# Great to be alive (1)

I am not an ace,
But I know how to do things at my pace.
I am not a magician,
But in certain things can beat a mathematician.

I am not rich,
But try to do on time my stitch.
I am doing all right.
It's a great day to be alive and to enjoy light!
*Sunday*                                    *11.10.2015*

# Rejoice (2)

Rejoice as many as God gave you years of youth.
Rejoice and also be as faithful as Ruth.
There is time for sadness, then be sad.
In the meanwhile, be happy and glad.

*Tuesday*                    *18.07.2017*


# Show me just a little smile

Please do not be upset,
Show me just a little smile.
I know, we've never met,
But we're on the same isle.

I've got a message for you:
Show me just a little smile.
Although far, you are close to me, it's true,
So, you're not alone; I like your kind style!

*Sunday*                    *16.07.2006*


# Great to be alive (2)

It is great to be alive!
I am so happy to see the blueness of the sky,
To contribute to a charitable bottle drive,
And to hear birds singing and to watch them fly.

I have hardships, true,
But as long as I keep on going,
Those can be worked through.
The advice is: keep on glowing.

*Saturday*                    *08.04.2017*


# Every day's a new life

Every day's a new life,
I can start from the beginning.
A wonderful chance to renew the strife,
The tune will be winning.

Each morning's a wonder,
Look better around.
What a beauty, even a thunder!
A singing bird… – what a sweet sound!

*Saturday*                    *05.04.2017*


# Rejoice before God

Rejoice before God in all!
He is Father of the fatherless and Judge of the widow indeed!
He hears when we call.
He helps in every good deed.

Rejoice before God in all!
Put sorrow without a reason away.
With God you will climb over any type of a wall!
In any situation you'll see bright day!

*Tuesday*                    *31.03.2015*


# Life is new

Life is new,
Life is fresh,
Life is indescribable!

Every morning brings new life,
I wake up and live anew.
I am brave to face a strife,
I am glad to see the dew.

One morning -> one more hope,
I am so lucky to live,
Friendship and love are in scope,
We will win, I believe.

Thank You Father for life!

*Saturday*                    *06.03.2010*

# Happy for the human race

When you are looking at a person sometimes,
You are happy for the human race –
I hope you can relate to these rhymes.
I hope you can be such an example in your own place.

*Thursday*                              *16.03.2017*


# How wonderful life can become

How wonderful life can become
If you are ready for this.
Your efforts are needed, yes, at least some,
Be willing to win and you will not miss.

This is not just my word,
But mine, of course, too.
Life is sharp, sometimes like a sword,
But much depends upon you!

*Sunday*                              *10.02.2008*


# Be happy (2)

"Be happy", they say,
But they lie:
"Watch TV, don't pray;
Going to Church, why",

They proclaim;
But the truth is:
Without God we miss the aim.
Think carefully, please.

*Sunday*                    *02.10.2016*


# Why are you so sad, o my soul?

Why are you so sad, o my soul?
Hope in God for I will give thanks to Him with an eager heart!
He is my salvation.
He makes me whole.
He is the wealth and defence of a nation.

*Friday*                    *17.06.2016*


# Do I still have the wisdom

Do I still have the wisdom
To be happy about little things?
Can I still spread my little wings;
Listen to a running stream without boredom;

Smell fresh air, flowers;
See the blueness of the sky,
The greenness of the grass growing by;
Marvel at ancient towers?

Oh, I think I do.
I just forget sometimes.
Thank Thee, Father, for these rhymes.
Thank Thee for taking me through!


# Don't be unhappy, I appreciate you

Don't be unhappy, I appreciate you
With all your strengths and weaknesses, true.
You are the apple of my eye;
You are the one of whom I never have enough, but I try.

*Wednesday*                    *28.12.2016*


# Don't let your sadness go too far

Don't let your sadness go too far –
There is a measure in all.
Don't be upset over spilt milk from a jar,
Say "forgive me" and bring down the wall.

If you had a quarrel today,
Do all you can to repair:
Give back, support, comfort, pray…
Only avoid despair.

*Monday*                    *12.12.2016*

# How to be happy

Be happy – the shortest and the only way is Christ.
Direct your ways to Him in all:
At home, at work, at leisure…
Let your kind deeds be filled with pleasure.
Keep Him in sight in winter, spring, summer, and fall.
Praise Him as if tomorrow may never come –
Say those kind words, do kind deeds, keep calm.

*Tuesday*                              *04.10.2016*


# What you have, hold

What you have, hold.
You are so rich indeed!
You are smart, you are bold,
Your health is more precious than gold.

So, be wise to save it and maintain.
No one knows what will happen then.
Under the sun or pouring rain,
Be sage to keep what is main.

Believe, these words are true.
You will need much strength –
Till the sky above is blue –
To do kind things, to break through!

*Sunday – Monday*                    *11-12.01.2009*

# Kindly smart

If it doesn't stick, bud,
Use a tape around that part.
If a car has passed and got you in mud,
Take it easy, be kindly smart.

Remember to run –
This is to cover your winning mile.
Remember to enjoy fresh air, bright sun.
Remember to smile =)

*Sunday*                              *25.09.2016*


# Learn to be happy about little things

Learn to be happy about little things,
Let not small trouble cut your wings.
Thank for what you have already
And fight to get other things ready!

*Sunday*                              *14.10.2012*


# Never! Never be shy to display your smile

Never! Never be shy to display your smile,
There is no use crying over spilt milk.

So, show your own free and simple style –
Your smile is softer than silk.

*Saturday*                    *18.12.2004*


# Cheer up, don't be upset

Cheer up, don't be upset,
You're strong and young.
How many miracles you haven't seen yet!
Come on, find and learn your tongue!

Don't allow yourself to be sad
About unimportant things
Because this state is rhymed to "mad",
Melancholy can only clip your wings.

*Saturday*                    *02.04.2005*


# Not much is required to be happy indeed

Not much is required to be happy indeed:
To love God sincerely in word and in deed,
To respect our neighbour truly,
And to do all things with love, honestly, and fully.

*Tuesday*                    *26.04.2016*

# Enjoy your life

Enjoy your life,
From dawn to set.
You are alive;
Don't get upset.

You are alive,
It means you'll do.
Your hope and love
Are brisk and true.

*Thursday – Friday*          *29-30.04.2010*


# The only way to multiply joy

The only way to multiply joy
Is to share it with others;
To do a kind deed
And to make happy your sisters and brothers.

*Sunday*          *10.01.2016*


# Rejoice (3)

However much you pray,
Rejoice, live life to the fullest each day.
Regardless of how much you fast, rejoice.
In anything you do, refine your choice.

Whatever you do, add love to it:
If you sew a suite, cut enough love to make a good fit;
If you make a salad, sprinkle it with love to perfect the taste;
If you write a computer code, insert love to go beyond copy and paste.

*Monday – Tuesday*                    *28-29.12.2015*


# Be happy (3)

However much you pray or fast,
Be happy! The days before have passed.
If you fast and pray a lot, be happy,
If you do just little, keep on snappy!

*Friday*                    *21.08.2015*

# STUDIES & WORK

## Salt and light

You are the salt of the earth truly.
You are the light of the world indeed.
Live up to these words of our Saviour fully.
Smile and with caution and wisdom proceed.

*Monday*                    *18.03.2019*


## Cool, patient and wise

Did you know that rage
Is a short-term madness?
It takes away the ability to be sage
And adds a lot of sadness.

Be able to control your emotions
Without any complex notions.
Just stay cool and wise,
Be patient, relax, awesomize.

*Monday*                    *18.03.2019*

# Talent

Did you know that talents are real,
And you have them too?
They can help get over an ordeal
And ensure you break through.

God bestows talents on us…
Would you use any as an expression of your gratitude
Showing your love to Him and your neighbour thus,
A thing that's a must in true Christian attitude?

*Wednesday*                    *13.03.2019*

# Address all important things in due course

It is easy to lose track of time,
And it is often a scarce resource.
Therefore, while you are still in your prime,
Address all important things in due course.

*Wednesday*                    *13.03.2019*

# Affordable asset

Is a must to win a deal;
Is an aid to succeed;

An asset to get a project done without any appeal;
A spice to flavour a meal;

A gulp of water to help cover a mile;
A great support in need;
A beautification to any style –
This simply is a sincere smile.

*Monday*                                     *04.03.2019*


# To worriers

Don't take yourself too seriously, friend;
And don't try to do all things right the first time.
Sometimes it's better to do and then to amend;
And when you work, do it with measure, otherwise, it can be a
crime.

*Sunday*                                     *03.03.2019*


# Haste makes waste

Haste makes waste.
Try to avoid hurrying:
This helps keep away from worrying.
This adds charm and taste!

*Sunday*                                     *10.03.2013*

# Wisdom of a situation

God put you in your current position –
Within it, be ready for unexpected things
And act boldly without waiting for a permission;
Pray each day to enjoy the fruits that wisdom brings.

*Sunday*                                    *10.02.2019*


# Practise patience and exercise caution

Practise patience and exercise caution
In air, on earth, on ocean.
This will give you an advantage over some others
And is of great use to all: hard workers, teachers, mothers…

*Wednesday*                                    *23.01.2019*


# Be gentle
Be gentle in all your ways:
In studies, work, with a dog;
During good and bad days;
At home, with buddies, when it's sunny, when there is fog.

If you don't, you will regret,
You'll wish you'd been gentle indeed,
You and your neighbour will be upset.
If you miss the mark, repent in word and deed.
*Tuesday*                                    *18.09.2018*

118

# If you want to succeed, watch your time

If you want to succeed, watch your time,
For the watchful, it brings juice, for the unwise, – a lime.
These rhymes are used to draw attention;
Remember about the early bird, what else to mention…?

*Sunday*                                    *22.04.2007*


# Like an olive tree

Rely on God to overcome worries –
He will establish you like an olive tree, just do your part
And leave the rest to God, the Manager of our life stories;
He heals our body, soul and heart.

*Friday*                                    *07.12.2018*


# Rely on God and act!

Rely on God and act!
Be wise and quick to react!
Let little misfortunes not discourage you.
Rely on God, even from fire He delivers and sends dew!

*June*                                      *2012*

# Never be sorry

Never be sorry
That you have missed,
Because if you do, you will worry –
This damages health and makes your mind wonder in mist.

Instead, thank God for all;
Do everything you can in the right direction.
While you live, you can do **any** correction.
Rely on God, don't drop the ball.

*Monday*                    *29.10.2018*


# When we do right things

When we do good things,
Other positive matters follow;
When we divert or fold our wings,
We find our victories lacking or hollow.

*Wednesday*                    *20.04.2011*


# Avoid wasting time
One of the biggest issues in the modern society
Is wasted time and a wish of quick prosperity.
Dedicate three hours a day to the cause you care,
Be sure, it will prosper, – keep your business fair.
*Sunday*                    *21.10.2018*

# By work and sufficient rest

How to achieve success?
By hard work and sufficient rest,
Pay attention more, not less.
Have time for break and work with zest.

*Friday*                    *21.10.2018*


# Do not be envious of a lawless man

Do not be envious of a lawless man:
He will be plucked out like grass;
His business will be under ban;
His inner world is amass.

*Sunday*                    *17.07.2017*


# Public speaking

If you have a hard time
Making a public presentation,
Think about the audience as if they owed you a dime;
Leave the rest to practice and preparation.

*Tuesday*                    *09.10.2018*

# Make hay while the sun shines

Make hay while the sun shines –
Do all things you can at once.
If you're writing a book, add to it each day new lines;
If you are a farmer, make sure all your cattle always receive a
health check glance.

Success comes from steady work
And dextrous hands.
These are the things making abundant your fork,
This is what gives fame to honest music bands.

*Friday*                                    *28.09.2018*


# One task at a time

In work or in studies,
There may be such times
When you need a hand from your buddies,
When clients are giving you limes.

Do not worry, do not despair.
Stay cool, be fair.
Tackle one task at a time;
Make juice of any lime.

*Friday*                                    *28.09.2018*

# Time for yourself

Have time for yourself each day.
Dedicate it to God; get creative, play;
Put aside your phone and computers far away;
Read, relax, cook, dream, plan, pray.

*Monday*                    *24.09.2018*


# Smile helps

Smile is what helps cover an extra mile.
Small or big, let it be sincere in all.
Share it with your friend and neighbour in winter frost and summer glare.
Smile and it will shine the way and help remain agile.

*Friday*                    *21.09.2018*


# All things are good in measure

All things are good in measure;
And too much of one thing is good for nothing, truly.
Enough work, a little leisure…
A bit of sadness, enough of happiness with gratitude fully.

Thursday                    13.09.2018

# Do first important things

If you want success,
Do first important things.
You'll wear a crown and nothing less,
Your fingers will have rings.

Do first important things,
Forget the fuss of every day.
Spread in confidence your wings!
What does the Bible say?

*Friday*                    *11.03.2011*


# For every kind deed you will get more

For every kind deed you will get more.
Do not expect from men,
In God be sure.
Have salt in yourself both now and then!

*Saturday*                    *05.03.2011*


# Smile
As often as possible, smile
And let your face be sincere.
Whether you're delivering a speech or installing a tile,
Smile, let it be full, not mere.
*Monday*                    *27.08.2018*

# Rely on God in all you deeds

Rely on God in all your deeds,
Rely on God in all your thoughts
And you will not crop weeds,
You will avoid many faults.

*Saturday*                                   *04.02.2012*

# Attentive prayer

Sometimes I get so busy
That in prayer I am far away.
Lord, let me stay focused although it ain't easy;
Let me believe, love, and pray.

*Sunday*                                     *06.05.2018*

# Prayer

Prayer is our support –
It protects, blesses, strives to comfort.
It is like a spiritual sport.
Use it in your business of any sort.

*Thursday*                                   *09.08.2018*

# Never stop creating

Never stop creating good, Christian things:
Let simple deeds of love and compassion help you spread your wings.
By doing nothing we learn to do ill:
Season with the salt of faith and hope your will.

*Sunday*                    *29.04.2018*


# To surrender is to lose more

Anyone can profit from good.
But turning misfortune to benefit
Is for the wise, I conclude.
Wisdom and patience cook their food.

To do well when all is okay
Is easy for our brain,
But in our heads we have much more than clay –
So, think what for. You can do it today.

To surrender when something is wrong,
To sink and to lose all
Or to step over and to try to become strong;
To save and to improve what you can so long?

It is up to you to decide;
Every new day is a beginning.
Birds know this, they do not hide.
In the open sky they glide.
*Sunday*                    *18.01.2009*

# One hour in the morning is worth three

One hour in the morning, friend,
Is worth three in the eve,
Whether you begin an activity or end,
Whether you come or leave.

Therefore, do what's important early in the day –
Add a step toward your dream;
Do morning exercises, pray.
Live, be happy, gleam.

*Sunday*                              *10.06.2018*


# Be wise

Be wise
And let your heart be firm,
So little time to realize,
Open your heart to learn.

*Tuesday*                              *14.07.2009*


# Never knowing what is ahead

Never knowing what is ahead,
Where you'll lose, where you'll find.
Never stubborn, always wiser instead
Keeping good things on your mind.

127

What you've got, hold,
Even more, multiply!
Cultivate good in yourself being bold.
Enable your heart and brain to amplify.

And me, I am with you.
How much we can save!
How beautiful are flowers in dew!
It is time to be brave!

*Sunday*                                    *01.06.2008*


# Just start

Rely on God with all your heart.
Do what is good;
Just start!

Continue achieving your goal.
Keep yourself busy with this
For this will replenish your bowl.

Just start!
Do not look back.
Rely on God with all your heart.

*Saturday*                                  *29.10.2006*

# Wit

Friend, God has given you wit –
Remember to use it.
In work and studies – apply to make a good fit.
Wisdom, faith, and courage make a good kit.

*Sunday*                    *15.04.2018*


# You get what you give

You get what you give,
Make sure you share good stuff.
Also make sure that you live,
That you work, that you love, that you laugh.

*Monday*                    *20.02.2017*


# Good and wise

Father, let Your slave be good and wise;
Let him rely on You in any situation.
Let him call on Your Name at noon, at night, at the sunrise.
Let him navigate to You in the age of information.

*Friday*                    *07.07.2017*

# Recipe

Take your passion,
Mix with hard work.
Clean and neat are always in fashion.
Keep mixing with a confident fork.

Add love as much as it takes.
Sprinkle generously with faith everywhere.
Add some hope before it bakes.
Remember to oil with rest; avoid despair.

*Monday – Tuesday*                    *09-10.04.2018*


# Starting all over

Don't be afraid to start
From the beginning –
Like Job did as God put it to his heart –
Despite all uncertainties towards which you may be leaning.

Your song will be winning;
Your reward will be great;
Your family will join you in singing;
You will pass many although you have come late.

*Monday*                    *06.11.2017*

# Reveal your way to the Lord

Reveal your way to the Lord,
Hope in Him and together you will do it!
He Who is the Greatest Reward
Will help, but act with wit.

*Sunday*                         *17.07.2016*


# Faith saves

Remember what Jesus Christ said to the blind,*
The leper and the Canaanite woman truly?
They made up their mind
To stick to faith, and He healed and helped them fully.

Do you also remember the widow's persistence –
Although the unrighteous judge showed resistance,
He helped after all.
Now let us also go and stick to faith in all!

*Blind – see Mark 10:46-52
Leper – see Mark 17:11-49
Canaanite woman – see Matthew 15:21-28
Widow (parable) – see Luke 18:1-8

*Sunday*                         *25.02.2018*

# Think you can do nothing, think again

When things do not work out and it looks all rain –
Think you can do nothing about it, think again!
There are A LOT of things you can do, but beginning is prayer.
Hard as things may seem, this brings you up like a stair.

*Sunday*                    *30.04.2017*


# Saving time on the Church or prayers

Have you ever tried
Saving time on the Church or prayer?
I have, trying to keep my eyes open wide,
To do more work, to add another successful layer.

When I skipped the Church to do work,
It didn't stick together, I had to redo;
I had or witnessed a quarrel over things as small as a fork;
I wasted time on much ado.

When I skipped prayers to do more,
I was unable to gain any time;
On the contrary, I lost to it another score;
I lost a dollar trying to save a dime.

I know other people who had similar situations.
Each of us is free to choose.
For me, the Church is a place of refuge in any nation
And prayers help to gain time, not to lose.
*Tuesday*                    *30.05.2017*

# Be patient in all important things

Be patient in all important things.
This means – do not worry.
However much waiting life brings;
However much trial and error – do not be sorry.

You can make corrections along the way.
However hard or busy – remember to pray.
Small as this thing may seem –
It will help approach your dream.

*Thursday*                    *20.07.2017*


# Keep your kind dream in sight!

Keep your kind dream in sight!
Keep working, perhaps, it is within a byte.
Perhaps, you'll need more work, more thinking power…
Pray on; keep it simple; dedicate to it the morning hour.

*January*                    *2018*


# Awesomize

Have faith, have strength to smile.
You are kind, be brave.
If necessary, wait for a while;
Be not afraid of a ranging wave.

For your Creator you are equal.
Be careful though and be wise.
Believe to add a happy ending to this sequel.
Get over, smile, and work to awesomize!

*Sunday*                                        *01.09.2013*


# Wrong or right?

For some you will always be of a wrong size:
Too small for some; too big for others at the same time.
Yet for others you will be just right – however hard to realize –
Even if you have a few extra pounds or as slim as a dime.

For some you will be a boor,
But for others – all right,
Whether you are rich or poor;
Their friend, gentle and bright.

Therefore, you will hear all,
But take things with a pinch of salt.
In all things pray, whether big or small.
Avoid those who do not love and find fault.

*Sunday*                                        *10.12.2017*

# You are not lazy

You are not lazy,
But your body needs rest.
In studies and work it does get crazy –
You need a break to perform best.

*Thursday*                    *27.04.2017*


# Prayer and time

When I pray, I have more time
To fulfill my tasks, to compose a rhyme.
It seems you lose minutes when you pray –
Believe, you gain hours and a day.

*Monday*                    *09.10.2017*


# I feel good whatever they say

I feel good whatever they say.
I'm all right, what a wonderful day!
I believe I can fly, I have wings
And I'll be a success; I'll improve the things.

*Sunday*                    *30.05.2004*

# Your smile

Smile and let your neighbour smile in return,
Let your smile help shine the way.
However much you need to learn,
Let your smile brighten the day!

*Tuesday*                    *03.10.2017*


# Dedicate mornings to important things

Dedicate mornings to important things,
Use evenings and spare time for shopping and less important
stuff.
Dedicate your strongest time that morning brings
To your important deeds, be blessed in them and sleep enough.

*Tuesday*                    *03.10.2017*


# Keep on working

Keep on working
However hard it is.
You will soon be "forking";
But now have patience, please.

The darkest hour
Is right before the dawn

You are this city's flower.
To get the prize we have to work hard like an ant and a prawn.

*Sunday*                                    *15.09.2013*

# Remain your kind self in any situation

Remain your kind self in any situation:
In an airport, at home,
At school, at work, during a presentation;
From Tivoli all the way east to Rome!

*Thursday*                                  *10.08.2017*

# Students

Students work hard,
But they work with hope
And in order not to be caught off guard.
As many assignments as given by profs, they cope.

However difficult, students keep on going
Because they know that their reward is awaiting –
For now, they have to be rowing.
God knows what good things in the future they will be
contemplating!

*Sunday*                                    *20.10.2013*

# Cheer and consistency

Do things with cheer
And your work will go far, not near.

But what has to be done – is to be done –
Do that and it will be gone.

Even famous people had tough times,
But continued working until they got juice out of limes.

Complete your kind projects through –
That's a rewarding thing, it's true.

*Saturday*                              *05.09.2015*


# People tend to put off important things

People tend to put off important things,
But be wise to do them at once, as if you had wings.
Then, maybe, God will bless you
Because He helps those who help themselves – it's true.

*Sunday – Monday*                        *03-04.03.2013*


# Why did you stop?

Why did you stop?
You are strong enough

To reach the top.
It's OK, let them laugh –

You'll score your goal.
Do what's on your mind,
You've got a friendly soul,
It's your day don't be blind.

*Saturday*                              *21.02.2004*


# Stay bright

Never give up the fight.
Keep on doing wise and kind things.
Your words and deeds can be like salt and light.
Only God knows what the future brings,

But you keep on rowing!
Whatever they say,
Keep on going!
With God's help you will succeed on your way!

*Tuesday*                               *01.11.2014*


# When you are studying for a degree

When you are studying for a degree,
Believe, you can achieve!

If you are tired of studying, plant a tree.
Continue rowing, till you receive!

*Sunday*                          *26.04.2015*


# Believe to achieve

There is so much you can achieve!
I know, it's hard to embrace,
But at any point believe,
Whether on earth or in space.

*Saturday – Sunday*              *18-19.04.2015*


# Work and Rest

If your work lasts 8 hours,
Work and then have rest.
Have time for your friends and for flowers,
Have time for play, and work with zest.

*Tuesday*                        *28.02.2017*


# Life is good

Life is good
Because it's a flow.

It is like trees in a wood:
Never the same wherever we go.

Where there is no loss,
There is no gain.
Misfortunes remind about victory's worth.
No exercises is starvation for brain.

A load is needed to make steel from muscles.
Without work a good gear rustles.
So, life is great forever!
Live and learn, be clever.

*Monday – Wednesday*          *05-07.05.2008*


# Why should I save what I received, what I've got?

Why should I save what I received, what I've got?
It's likely to go bad, it's likely to rot.
Isn't it better to invest
In order to get the best?

You can understand what I say.
Be attentive while it's light, while it's day.
I'm speaking about talents rather than money.
Think and do good stuff while it's sunny.

*Sunday*          *26.03.2005*

# Perennial values

Sometimes she makes mistakes.
It's natural, it's alright.
Nevertheless, her young heart aches.
She's a modern girl and is always ready to fight.

She works hard
And can never forgive herself a blunder.
They say, "It's a normal state of things, dear bard.
Calm down, we need no thunder".

How can it be OK
If she has no time for her family and friends?
Her work is a beast and she is a prey.
Pure soul is the treasure, but not what money sends.

*Saturday*                    *26.03.2005*


# Read & run

Read 'cause reading will make you wise,
Your intelligence is very likely to rise.
In the Wise Book, you will find answers.
Your ideas will be as swift as lancers.

Run to do good and kind things;
Be quick and light as if with wings.
In all things avoid haste:
It certainly makes waste.
*Thursday*                    *05.02.2015*

# Don't be afraid of making a repairable mistake

Don't be afraid of making a repairable mistake:
To take a university course, to meet a friend, to buy a car of a wrong make...
You will sincerely apologize, you will earn that extra dime.
The thing is you thought you have time.

*Saturday*                    *11.02.2017*

# Keep your dreams alive

Keep your dreams alive,
Cherish them in spite of all.
However long is the drive,
Listen to your heart's call.

*Monday*                    *17.05.2010*

# Good dreams

Not only dream your good dreams,
But also pursue them.
However hard it seems –
Keep going toward your gem.

*Tuesday*                    *17.01.2017*

# What for are you asking 'why'

What for are you asking 'why'?
You'd better ask 'how'.
Spread your mind and fly.
You can improve the things right now.

Life is too short to look back.
Of course, you can moan and yelp,
But unique is your track.
Love and confidence will endure and help.

*Friday*                              *02.01.2009*


# Time is sly indeed

Time is sly indeed,
It's moving faster day after day.
Who knows what I need?
What shall I say?

Anyway, never stop rowing,
Keeping heart open;
Never being afraid of bestowing.
That is the only way in order not to feel broken.

What for to put off till tomorrow
A kind smile, a good deed?
Retardation leads to sorrow.
Time is sly indeed.
*Tuesday – Wednesday*              *12-13.12.2006*

# What if you earn that amount

What if you earn that amount
Because you are expected to share a part?
Be willing to give from your account
Out of love and to succeed in every good start.

*Wednesday*                    *02.11.2016*


# What if whatever you earn

What if whatever you earn
Is so much to be able
To share, to stay healthy, to learn,
To fill a poor man's table?

Imagine, what if by doing these things
You fulfill His will,
You help spread somebody's wings,
You help pay that important bill?

What if by being faithful in few things
You will be blessed with much more to carry on with good stuff
Even with your wedding rings, –
Your second half to help you in all and when it gets rough?

*Wednesday*                    *02.11.2016*

# Avoid putting blame

Avoid putting blame –
It makes a person lame;
It stirs a burning flame;
It doesn't help to win a game.

*Sunday*                    *22.10.2016*


# Let your light smile shine the way

Let your light smile shine the way.
Let your kind words make the day.
Be your gentle self everywhere
Because you love, because you care.

*Friday*                    *14.10.2016*


# Greed makes blind

Greed makes seeing eyes blind,
And hearts become a selfish stone;
It lays fat on mind.
Greed leaves people lonely and alone.

*Sunday*                    *04.10.2009*

# Be yourself whatever they say

Be yourself whatever they say,
Don't be under anybody's thumb.
They want you to go? How about you stay?
You're strong without any rum.

It's not easy, but try to smile
And don't be afraid to display your knowledge –
That'll help you to cover thousands of miles;
Be yourself at home, at work and at college.

*Saturday*                              *05.06.2004*


# With faith

Best things in life
Happened when God blessed me to act with faith indeed:
Success in studies, finding wife,
Seeing far-away places, happiness, conquering greed.

Bad things are preceded
By absence of faith in deeds:
Bad luck at work, lack of support when it is needed,
Worry, abundance of effort with many unsprouted seeds.

*Monday*                                *05.09.2016*

# Laughter is the answer

Sometimes laughter is the answer in a situation
If things all, but stick together in a conversation.
When something happens and you do not know how to react,
Just smile and proceed with tact.

*Monday*                         *05.09.2016*


# How important it is to be sure (1)

How important it is to be sure,
And to have wisdom in store!
It will bring much courage, success,
You will know what to answer, when to say "no" and when to
say "yes".

*Sunday*                         *30.03.2008*


# To act upon consideration

To act upon consideration
Involves patience and confidence without hesitation.
This lays the way to success in all.
Wisdom will make peaceful your station.

You will have no call.
Patience will save you from a fall.

Wisdom… The whole world is in this word,
It can heal, it can fly, it can crawl!

*Sunday*                    *02.03.2008*


# Patience is all we need

Patience is all we need!
To savour sweet berries
A farmer takes a small seed.
But time is not sold like cherries.

He who knows how to wait
Inherits riches and fame.
Better wise now than when it is too late;
Learn to control your flame.

Open your eyes to avoid blindness.
Here are two words to learn by heart:
Patience and kindness.
Among the great they make your part.

*Saturday – Sunday*              *16-17.02.2008*


# By being passive, you learn to lose

By being passive, you learn to lose.
How easy it is just to snooze:

No struggle, no run, no winning bell...
It's only then that you will regret, "I could have won, but fell".

So watch where you go
While it's not too late, while you can row.
There are two ways, it's up to you to choose:
Either to win or to lose.

*Monday*                    *06.03.2006*


# Eliminate worry

Rely on God to eliminate worry.
I know you believe, but let your faith show in deed.
He crowns His flock with glory.
He is with us in every need.

*Sunday*                    *14.08.2016*


# When did you last admire the sky?

When did you last admire the sky,
Green grass, and strong trees?
This is amazing, try!
You are required no fees.

How often do you look far away?
Ask yourself. The question is why.

What for to leave when you want to stay?
What for to cut your wings if you can fly?

Vanity is nothing,
Money is only a means.
Look at those who are constantly fussing.
Already old being in their teens!

But we still have a chance.
Your time hasn't yet slept away.
Always moving like in a dance...
What is there ahead in your way?

*Wednesday*                              *01.08.2007*


# Time is slipping away

Time is slipping away.
Can you try to make it stay?

Nobody can, I presume.
Time escapes leaving reflections like an expensive perfume.

Always searching for better...
Always striving to read life's enveloped letter...

Time is short and days are few.
Obscure or obvious, but it's true.

To share time among best things
Is like a bird that flies and sings.

Wisdom makes good use of days.
He'll win who listens to what it says.

*Monday*                                    *09.03.2009*


# The grass isn't always greener

The grass isn't always greener
On the other side of the fence!
I hope you've noticed the screamer!
And I've meant no offence.

Just look better around,
Keep carefully what you own.
It'll make your body sound,
And your soul will throw away the stone.

Be proud of your garden
And take care of it.
Wisdom is the best guard
And it'll help you a bit.

*Saturday*                                  *06.11.2004*


# Do not be envious of him who does lawless things

Do not be envious of him who does lawless things –
He fulfills his own whim, he cuts his own wings.

God sees to repay each one according to their deeds –
Nothing is hidden from Him under the sun: good fruit and
weeds.

*Saturday – Sunday*                    *18-19.06.2016*


# All work and no play

All work and no play
Makes Jack a dull boy.
Cool down, it's your day,
Try to smile and jump for joy.

*Saturday*                    *31.01.2004*


# Strengthen your heart

Strengthen your heart
And wait on the Lord with patience.
He crowns with victory your finish and blesses your start.
He makes your name known among nations.

*Wednesday*                    *08.06.2016*

# Rely on God whatever

Rely on God whatever,
You will not regret ever.
Your face will shine.
Your business will thrive!

*Sunday*                                *04.03.2012*


# When you have so many things to do

When you have so many things to do,
Try one at a time,
This may be better for you.
I tried to put it in rhyme.

*Sunday*                                *31.10.2010*


# Whatever you do – add love to it

Whatever you do – add love to it
To make your work a perfect fit.
Just do your job with love indeed:
Let your love be seen in word and in deed.

*Saturday*                              *02.04.2016*

# I wish I had never hesitated

I wish I had never hesitated,
Just always pushed forward, never waited.
Then I would have escaped so much trouble,
I would have gained double.

But all the same, it's all right
'Cause my mistakes are in sight
And that's the first stage:
'To realize' is the foregoer of 'to become sage'.

I'm going to be sure when doing good
And also firm when saying 'no' to bad or rude.
That's the way to be
For those who want to win, for thee.

*Friday*                                   *10.03.2006*


# What you can do to succeed, do

What you can do to succeed, do, –
Put off secondary things to free your head;
Remember what is true,
In order to fly keep your wings spread.

*Sunday*                                   *23.10.2011*

# Rely on God in all you do

Rely on God in all you do
And let your heart be calm.
Out of all He will deliver you;
You and yours will suffer no harm.

A thousand and ten thousand will fall beside you,
But to you they won't break through
Because you called God your Helper truly.
He will make you thrive, He will protect you fully.

*Thursday*                    *17.03.2016*

# If things do not stick

If things do not stick together,
Patience, it will soon pass.
You will spread your beautiful wings feeling lighter than a
feather.
Fill up with patience as you fill up with gas.

*Monday*                    *29.02.2016*

# Smile, even if you work hard

Smile, even if you work hard,
Whether you eat veggies or lard,

All will be all right;
Keep victory in sight!

*Saturday*                           *20.02.2016*


# Balance

I know you go to Church a lot,
But how do you react when you see someone in need,
With fear and distrust or with a welcome which is hot,
With generosity or with greed?

Yes, you have to take care,
But you also have to be helpful, loving, and fair.
How to manage? Try balance in all,
Add a pinch of wisdom, sprinkle with love, go to Church, read the Scroll*.

* The Bible.

*Sunday*                             *14.02.2016*


# Ask Questions

Don't be shy to ask:
This makes clear your task;
This enables to help better
And to write a stronger letter.
*Sunday*                             *14.02.2016*

# How important it is to be sure (2)

How important it is to be sure!
No doubt on that score.
You need not hesitate,
Believe, till it's not too late.

You may try yourself anyway.
What else can I say?
I've tried, now I know:
So much time I felt low...

But you will enjoy success.
It's up to you: either more or less.
Be strong and keep within law,
How important it is to be sure!

*Sunday*                    *09.12.2007*


# With simplicity

Approach all matters with love and simplicity.
Filter all information with a grain of salt:
International affairs, technology, obesity...
Let your thinking process never halt!

*Tuesday*                    *25.11.2014*

# How do you use your time?

I know, you have so little time,
But it's all about how you use it.
Do you spend a dollar trying to save a dime?
If you are overwhelmed with details, you may lose it.

Keep the bigger picture in sight,
Approach it in a smart way indeed.
Your time budget is tight –
Be wise with time to succeed.

*Monday*                     *12.01.2015*

# Haste makes waste

Haste makes waste –
It's an easy thing to remember.
Sometimes you have to do more than just copy and paste;
It's a good thing to bear in mind from January through
December.

Avoid hurrying to look and be professional.
Your business will move more smoothly
And grow international.
Your decisions will be more rational.

*Tuesday – Wednesday*            *26-28.01.2015*

# Thank Thee Father for the exam

Thank Thee Father for the exam.
Thy help is a protective slam.
This exam, Thou passed it for me,
If Thou art close, I will never flee.

With Thee is the life,
I will stand in a strife.
Thank Thee for Thy precious support
Which is more than the best unassailable fort!

Thou give comfort, good luck,
In no bog I will be stuck;
Thou art with me,
Thy support makes us free!

*Friday – Sunday*        *21-23.12.2007*


# Best investment

First best investment is education,
It does not matter where you were born, to what nation.
Money gets cheaper each day –
Education will grow in price without delay.

Second best investment is your wife.
When it gets tough in life,
She will sell her jewellery to support the family: your children
and you.
Whatever the situation is, good or bad, keep your love true.

Third best investment is children indeed.
When the time comes, invest in their education, word, and deed.
When you grow old,
They will support you, among your neighbours you will be bold.

*Friday*                              *04.12.2015*


# Remember to play

You work hard, but remember to play,
To do good things you like whatever they say.
You are not lazy – your body needs rest.
This will help you to continue with zest.

*Wednesday*                           *11.11.2015*


# Faith and sweat

How to achieve our goals?
The answer is simple – faith and sweat.
This will take us far and replenish our bowls.
This will allow us to meet all the priorities that have been set.

*Wednesday*                           *11.11.2015*

# Make decisions

Decisions are a skill,
Make decisions and get better at it,
Whether they concern your food or bill.
Yes, you will have to apply all your wit.

At first you may make some mistakes,
But let it take what it takes.
Some decisions require a piece of advice.
So, be wise, practice, cut your slice.

*Saturday*                    *24.10.2015*


# Exercise your body

Exercise your body –
You only get one.
Whether you work or study,
There are a lot of things that can be done.

What do you like?
Walking, swimming, jogging or riding a bike;
Playing basketball, volleyball, soccer or dancing?
There are things which require no financing.

You have no time to spare;
In fact, exercising will save you some.
It will help you to learn, to work, and to prepare.
Find the exercises you like and come!
*Saturday*                    *24.10.2015*

# Educate yourself

A lot of things happen around
And it is not enough to learn what you are told at school.
New things, new technologies abound
And it takes an effort to stay cool.

Have desire to learn new things
To be able to choose what is good,
To be able to distinguish good stuff from unhealthy springs.
Be kind, smart, and learn to move ahead from where you stood.

*Saturday*                              *17.10.2015*


# Continue doing good stuff

Victories are not for good,
But we relax and lose the place where we stood:
We achieve one thing and stop
Instead of trying to make a longer hop.

Failures are not final
Even if the injury is spinal,
But we tend to give up after the first try
Whereas more effort we are to apply.

Remember to give a good cause another chance –
Be it in business or in romance;
Success is to be enjoyed and built upon.
Failures are to be endured and conclusions are to be drawn.
*Sunday*                              *27.09.2015*

# My students

My students are smart.
They may lack wisdom, but they are working on it;
They are making much progress, not just a bit.
To advance is what they have put to their heart.

Students are juice of economy in any city:
They are young and ready to work;
For them, job comes first and only then a spoon and a fork.
They work a lot and they are witty.

So teach students with appreciation;
Hire them for the best jobs as soon as you can.
They will help you to make a plan
To succeed and to advance your business among the whole
population.

*Saturday*                                    *19.09.2015*


# Be simple

Be simple and people will want to be with you.
It's not bad to look smart and gentle since it is true.
Do not be shy to display your knowledge;
Be simple, but do not forget what you have learned at college.

*Sunday*                                    *30.11.2014*

# Think before you answer

Always think before you answer,
Take your time to reflect.
You are not a break dancer;
Think now because your reply will have an effect.

*Saturday*                    *01.11.2014*


# Birthday

It is your birthday today,
And I don't know what to wish, you have all.
Just a couple of things: you work hard, but remember to play.
When you are happy or sad, remember to pray.
*Friday*                         *21.08.2015*


# Time to do right

Do not listen to the one who is hurrying –
Have time to do it right –
Things for him are blurry,
But you keep clear sight.

*Thursday*                    *02.06.2011*

# You have a talent

You have a talent.
Those who cannot see are blind.
You are beautiful, you are smart, you are gallant.
Stay strong, keep open your mind.

When your talents will flourish like buds,
It will amaze all.
Your knowledge and talent will break through like spring
floods;
Your achievements will be discussed by scholars in a university
hall.

Stay strong, keep loving your heart;
Be nice whatever they say.
Be kind and joyful to start.
Work hard, study thoroughly, remember to play.

*Sunday*                    *28.06.2015*


# Learn to listen then you will see

Learn to listen then you will see,
You will understand clearer;
People will think wiser of thee.
Knowledge will become nearer.

*Friday*                    *19.06.2015*

# Except the Lord shall build the house

Except the Lord shall build the house,
They labour in vain that build it.
God protects against destruction, theft, and mouse.
God saves out of the deepest pit.

Except the Lord shall keep the city,
The watchman wakes up in vain.
God makes nation's leaders witty.
He cures our infirmities and multiplies the harvest of grain.

*Sunday*                          *21.06.2015*

# COURAGE

## Keep on going (1)

Love God with all your heart!
And do not doubt in any part.
God loved you from the beginning,
He wants to see you winning!

Allow your faith to guide you,
Let it shine like crystal dew,
Take love in all your ways:
It will prolong your days.

Believe in God and go!
Let your hope grow,
Let your light shine!
You are a grape – He is the Vine.

*Sunday*                              *07.10.2012*


## To avoid losing

A loss begins from the heart,
It then passes through the head
And the results start,
And the prevalent light becomes red.

To avoid losing
The best thing you can do

Is to begin with your heart, – what it is choosing.
Take good care of it and you will break through!

*Friday*                                    *22.02.2019*


# Through all your life length

Have courage, my friend,
In any situation till the very end!
Let your heart not faint,
Remember people who are saint!

God is with you!
You will break through.
Have courage and strength
Through all your life length.

*Sunday*                                    *13.01.2013*


# When life is not all smooth

When life is not all smooth,
Have head to keep on rowing!
God will restore the truth,
Your wisdom ought to keep showing!

*Monday*                                    *25.06.2012*

# Protect good

It's not enough to avoid evil things,
Neither is it enough to do good –
It is important to prevent evil from spreading its wings
And to defend the truth in a cheerful mood.

*Sunday*                              *06.01.2019*


# Whatever happens, stand! (1)

Whatever happens, stand!
The relief is near.
However hard to understand,
Open your heart to hear.

Your faith and hope, and love
Will bring you to the top.
From hand you'll feed a dove,
But now move on, no need to stop.

*Sunday*                              *25.10.2009*


# Each person has her/his own day

Each person has her/his own day.
Even if everyone around seems so smart,
Pay attention, keep doing the right thing the right way, pray.

Start with faith and humbleness that come from the heart. Use art.

Don't be envious, do not freak out.
Keep calm, be simple and wise.
Stout or slim, with a workout or without,
Awesomize; remember that steady wins the prize and he who tries.

*Saturday – Sunday*                    *17-18.11.2018*


# Explore, research, discover

Explore, research, discover
Whether you are a scholar or a music lover,
A Christian or still in search of the Way;
Whether you are a priest or lay.

In doing so, apply wit, enthusiasm and smile:
Your merchandise will be the first to clear the store aisle;
Your friendships will grow stronger;
Your health and happiness will abide longer.

*Monday*                    *05.11.2018*


# Evangelise

Evangelize, my friend:
Share the Church with others.

Remember Lazarus's and the rich man's end.
Share the Saviour with your sisters and brothers.

You were born in the Orthodox faith, you say?
Excellent, in faith you are rich like the rich man –
Out of your richness you are expected to pay.
Put any laze and unrighteous hesitation to ban.

You ask, what tools you have to start?
I ask, what else do you need?
You have two feet and a Christian heart,
You have the hungry flock to feed.

*Friday*                                    *09.11.2018*


# Hold your faith at all times

Hold your faith at all times
Although life may have presented limes…
Hold and keep on praying.
There is time for reflecting and time for playing.

Above all, stay in love that is true,
Let it get you all the way through!
Rely on God and go
And you will have good fruit to mow!

*Sunday*                                    *30.09.2012*

# Believe (1)

However hard, avoid despair.
Be sure, God is strong to repair.
However broken, believe
That when the time comes, you will receive.

Be simple and stand in hope.
Stock up with faith to cope.
Cherish love and abide in it.
Be strong, be friends with wit!

*Monday*                    *01.10.2018*


# Let good remain

We live, what can be better, in fact?
How much we can, ours is the time to react!
Always in search of the way.
Motion is life, wrong is delay.

It doesn't matter where I've been,
But where I'm going.
In spite of misfortunes I've seen,
I look ahead; a gentle wind is blowing.

No matter what will happen tomorrow,
I want to do good today.
It brings in light, takes away sorrow.
Love and kindness remain, whatever they say!
*Saturday*                    *19.07.2008*

# If you are in doubt

If you are in doubt,
Rely on God, colleague,
He makes our steps stout,
The tired continue without fatigue.

By following His word
You will go far,
His truth is a sword,
In darkness or light it shines from afar.

*Saturday*                    *28.01.2012*


# When you lose yourself

When you lose yourself in life,
Your courage will soon follow.
Keep good things however harsh is the strife.
Your success will come, your storehouses will not be hollow.

*Monday*                    *17.09.2018*


# Friends

Be friendly if you want to have friends.
Be friendly, despite misfortunes it will all settle in the end.
Be gentle, patient and loving in all everywhere.
Be courageous, discover and dare!
*Wednesday*                    *05.09.2018*

# There is a reason for you to be here

There is a reason for you to be here,
Abide in light!
The night is far, the day is near –
Keep that in sight!

*Thursday*                    *09.08.2018*

# The righteous shall flourish

The righteous shall flourish
Like a palm tree;
Like food and water that nourish –
They help to set free.

*Wednesday*                    *20.07.2016*

# No good deed is too small
No good deed is too small,
Whether it's picking up a glove,
Holding the door or being gentle on a phone call,
Whether it's feeding a man or a dove…

Be thankful for a good deed;
Accept gratitude with a gentle, shining smile too.
You are changing the world taking lead:
One good deed at a time, true.
*Wednesday*                    *18.04.2018*

# God's salvation

God's salvation
Is very close to those
Who fear Him in every nation –
To those who multiply faith, hope and love among population.

*Wednesday*                                    *20.07.2016*

# Living Christian

Being Christian doesn't mean
Living an easy life without limes –
It can get tough for all at times –
It means doing Christian things and growing up like a tree that's
green.

*Tuesday*                                    *14.03.2017*

# Have a heart and intelligence hold

Have a heart and intelligence hold;
Be loving, but also be smart.
Remember your Heavenly Father, be bold.
To win – do your part.

*Sunday*                                    *08.08.2010*

# Power, love, wisdom

Christians should act
Boldly in all good things
Because God did not give us the spirit of timidity, in fact,
He gave us the spirit of power, love, wisdom and the positivity it
brings.

*Saturday – Sunday*          *30.03-01.07.2018*

# Rely on God and boldly step ahead

Rely on God and boldly step ahead.
Let Him direct your way, let Him anoint your head;
Let Him remove your sorrow and let Him give you joy instead.
He is the One Who redeemed you, protected and fed.

*Friday*          *15.06.2018*

# Whatever has happened

Whatever has happened,
There is no reason for despair –
However hard or unfair.
Whatever has happened...

Everything will be all right.
D'you know why I am so sure?

I trust in God, His Law.
Everything will be all right!

*Sunday*                              *21.01.2012*

# You are important

Each of us is valuable truly.
Each of us is important fully.
Avoid thinking otherwise;
If needs be, do awesomize.

We are bought with the Precious Price:
Christ gave Himself for you and me by device.
Knowing this, go, believe and act.
You are important, it's a fact.

*Saturday*                            *28.04.2018*

# Nothing can separate us from God

Nothing can separate us from God at all.
Neither height, nor strength, nor circumstances whatsoever;
Neither a big thing, nor small.
The truth is He loves us and we love Him now and ever.

*Wednesday*                           *18.04.2018*

# Once I donated

Once I donated
Without expecting anything back.
I know that the giver's hand will not be underrated,
That s/he will not lack.

What I didn't know
Was that it would happen in no time.
Sometimes we plant and we have to wait for the seed to grow,
Whether we donate skills or a dime.

Be patient, have faith –
If bad stuff grows, more so the good;
Things happen at their own pace.
Good things are worth doing I'd like to conclude.

*June*                                    *2017*


# Strengthen your heart in God

Hope in God and let your heart
Strengthen in Him fully:
He will bless your start
And will ensure success of your completion truly.

*Monday*                          *04.09.2017*

# Keep on rowing

Whatever happens, keep on rowing.
If you are in doubt, keep on going.
If you are tired, take a break, you'll need it to continue glowing.
If you are a student, keep learning to keep on growing!

*Friday*                                    *30.06.2017*


# Smiling faith

You should believe in such a way
That your face is smiling,
Because Christ cares for you at night and at day.
Start sharing your faith and smile, stop compiling.

*Sunday*                                    *04.03.2018*


# Don't be afraid to make a mistake

Don't be afraid to make a mistake,
Whether you are thinking to invite your date to a lake,
Or whether you are trying out new things to bake.
Be courageous – this is a feature to never forsake!

*Friday*                                    *30.06.2017*

# Never settle for the path of least resistance

Never settle for the path of least resistance.
A lot of things have been achieved through persistence.
Don't be shy to use your family's loving assistance.
Pray and believe at all times and God will make you go a long
distance.

*Sunday*                                    *18.02.2018*


# Be brave, my friend

Be brave, my friend.
Rely on God and go ahead!
Your courage to success will lend.
To avoid loss, engage your head.

*Sunday*                                    *31.10.2010*


# You are with sad eyes

You are with sad eyes.
Courage, friend!
The sun will rise;
The day will come, the night will end.

*Wednesday*                                 *20.12.2017*

# Don't be afraid

However difficult is the situation –
Don't be afraid.
At work, at home, in studies, among a foreign nation...
God's love is with you, the problem will fade.

*January*                    *2018*


# Whatever happens, stand! (2)

Whatever happens, stand!
In air, on water, on land...
However hard or not right –
Do the correct thing, abide in light!

*January*                    *2018*


# Your smile :)

It is worth being able to smile
Because people often need it,
They will smile back
Together you will cover a thousand's mile;
Together you will reinforce your spirit.
Nothing will lack!

*Wednesday*                    *28.12.2011*

# Remain yourself

It is easy to lose,
To get lost in the cruise:
Waves are crying in rage.
Your way is to be sage.

Keep what is true,
Your love and faith,
Keep to come through.

God knows what is ahead.
But now be brave
And respect your intelligent head!

*Monday*               *21.12.2009*


# Never give up in any good deed

Never give up in any good deed,
Whether you are studying or pulling out a garden weed,
Whether you are writing a dissertation
Or working on a new invention.

Never give up in a good endeavour,
Be cheerful, hopeful, faithful, and clever.
For all good things pray.
May God's blessing help you each day!

*Tuesday 20.12.2005 – Saturday 28.01.2006*

# As much as you can

As much as you can, believe –
Let God tell you, "Your faith has saved you".
When it seems impossible to receive,
Believe and work hard with a rolled up sleeve.

*Sunday*                    *29.10.2017*


# Whatever happens

Whatever happens, life is going on.
Life… How much sense there is in the word!
Whatever life brings, it is worth moving on.
Look at a little bird…

So weak, fragile,
But it will live,
It will cover a mile,
It will, for sure, believe.

Life is a precious gift!
So much for others we can do.
No time for a drift.
Stop, just think, it's true.

*Wednesday*                    *26.11.2008*

# You will do!

You will do!
I am sure;
This poem is true.
No matter what is the score.

Just think,
How much you can!
Of course, not all in a wink,
To win is your plan!

You are clever,
Your chances are high!
Never say never...
Get ready and try!

*Saturday*                    *23.08.2008*


# Rely on God and go

Rely on God and go!
Let your spirits be high, not low.
Be confident because you did right.
Your face diffuses light.

While in the world you are,
Use wit to go far.
Be gentle and sage,
Do not be afraid of waves that rage!
*Sunday*                    *18.11.2012*

# Pray on

The darkest hour
Is before the dawn.
A bud comes before a flower;
Mud grows a beautiful lawn...

Your hope is your light,
Keep it in sight.
Your anchor is faith, true.
Love is your cleansing bath, keep it if you want to break
through.

*Tuesday*                    *17.10.2017*


# When I am in trouble, I pray

When I am in trouble, I pray
And then try to do all I can.
I can't explain the bright ray
Which crosses the gloom and improves my plan.

That's how we know God loves us all,
He hears each our call.
The Father and the Friend till the end of times,
It is beyond the rhymes...

His help is obvious and swift,
God helps us, it needs no seal.
Not unassisted, not by chance we get lift,
Let's keep our hearts open to feel.
*Tuesday*                    *22.05.2007*

186

# The sun will shine

The sun will shine,
The day will glow –
The night decline;
The light will grow!

*Sunday*                    *05.02.2012*


# Cheer up, don't worry!

Cheer up, don't worry!
Why are you so sad?
You will succeed, so hurry,
Keep on trying, what else can be said?

Strive and you'll do.
Seek and you'll find!
These words are true.
Minor problems? Never mind!

*Tuesday*                    *30.01.2007*


# Have faith to stand (1)
Have faith to stand.
Even when it is hard and you cannot understand,
Keep going and doing good things.
Have faith and spread your wings!
*Sunday*                    *06.07.2014*

# Believe in God and boldly step

Believe in God and boldly step,
Keep straight your awesome back!
Your pocket will not lack,
Your house will not crack

Because you called your God your Help,
Because you worked with hope.
Your business will certainly thrive,
Your household will be as full as a bee hive!

*Sunday*                              *20.07.2014*


# Keep trying

However hard and little luck,
Go on, keep on trying.
Perhaps, your success is behind next try, stuck.
Giving up hope is like dying.

Ask and you will receive.
Knock and they will open to you.
Good things require persistence, so do not leave.
Oh, how important it is to continue seeking, it's true.

+ See Matth. 7:7-8

*Sunday*                              *24.09.2017*

# Keep your chin kindly up

You are strong, believe and go.
Your Father is with you!
Be brave, what people can do?
Be sage, the seed of truth will grow.

*Saturday*                    *09.01.2010*


# Lord, help us and let the nations see

Lord, help us and let the nations see.
Let them fear God and give up their plea;
Let the evil repent in his heart.
Lord, help us and do not depart!

*Monday*                    *23.03.2015*


# Life of faith
Life of faith is when you live with love and believe,
While you still have nothing, that you will receive.
Life of faith is when you act with hope
That God will give you a Hand however steep is the slope.

Be of faith in life,
However rough is the strife.
Be of good cheer – God loves you;
Be wise and sober for it is true.
*Sunday*                    *10.09.2017*

# Live as if tomorrow never comes

We tend to live
As if we are here forever.
We keep things forgetting to give;
We tend to be thrifty rather than clever.

But what if tomorrow never comes?
What if God calls us today?
Do we realize to what our life sums?
Therefore, act boldly, remember to love and pray.

*Monday*                    *04.09.2017*


# Be courageous

Be courageous in work and studies;
Be courageous when you meet a lady or old buddies.
Be creative in doing good things.
Do all with love and see what fruit this brings!

*Sunday*                    *18.06.2017*


# Keep hope
However hard, keep hope;
Hold it at all times.
With your problems to cope,
Do not lose it even when you receive limes.
*Saturday*                    *02.07.2011*

# When you are in doubt: believe

When you are in doubt: believe
Be brave in order to achieve.
Be brave, you will receive.

*January*                    *2011*

# Forget your fears

Forget your fears,
You should be above them all;
Your problems aren't worth your tears,
God will pick you up after any fall.

Keep your back straight.
Let wisdom protect you.
Never say that it's too late –
You'll be given your due.

*Saturday*                    *09.10.2004*

# What does it mean to be a man?

What does it mean to be a man?
You should be sure to understand,
It's not easy, but, I believe, you can –
Be brave and wise: go, run, just never stand.

Is he strong? It's not enough,
Even if he has never cried,
It only makes him tough.
A man will never show false pride.

*Friday*                              *25.07.2017*


# Have strength to dream you kind dreams

Have strength to dream you kind dreams –
Even after you come through flames and streams –
Let your dreams be living –
For that purpose – keep trying and believing!

*Thursday*                            *13.07.2017*


# The night has passed

The night has passed,
The day has come
It's time to act and fast.
No need to be glum.

A new day means a new life.
So, be ready,
Today you'll have to face a strife.
Smile, be steady!

If something is wrong,
Work toward a change
Because you are strong,
And that is within your range.

*Sunday*                            *04.11.2007*


# There is no time for hesitation

There is no time for hesitation,
Choose your way and go.
There is no time for hesitation,
Choose your boat and row.

Soon you will see the sun appear
And it will lighten your way.
Kind Heart, your luck is near,
The night retreats, you will enjoy the day!

What for to look back?
Every step draws nearer your wonderful aim.
You will forget about lack.
You will win though the world is never the same.

Be confident, act;
Your garden will thrive!
Your shield is good tact.
Wisdom is with you wherever you drive.

*Thursday*                          *13.11.2008*

# Believe (2)

Believe as long as possible, believe.
It is always easy to leave –
Keep on trying, being persistent in good:
Studying, resting, praying, saying, working under a hood.

Be ready to say "no" to bad things
Because they will encapsulate your neck and nose with rings.
Before you answer, reflect and pray:
Give it a thorough test before you say.

*Monday –Tuesday*                    *09-10.02.2015*


# However hard it is, go on

However hard it is, go on.
I know problems weigh much,
But to win you were born;
Your kind heart makes you strong as such!

It's never too late to improve
When you are ready to fight,
Your deeds will prove,
You will enjoy a victorious light.

But now be patient to wait, let the day chase night.
What cannot be cured,
Should be endured.
A climber starts from the bottom to reach the height.
*Sunday*                    *13.01.2008*

# If life deceives

If life deceives,
Don't get upset:
Only its sons it receives.
Your task will be half done as soon as it is set!

Smile, my friend!
Rely on God on all occasions.
Keep faith till the end,
Whether among Europeans or Asians!

*Sunday*                    *04.03.2012*


# When you are sad

When you are sad,
Take your time,
Get ready to be glad.
Make juice if you got a lime.

Remember to smile,
It helps with people.
They will appreciate your style.
You can make much even out of little.

*Friday*                    *21.05.2010*

# Somehow you will

When you believe,
Miracles happen indeed.
However hard in work or other deed,
Somehow you will!

*Wednesday*                    *22.04.2015*


# Every child has a kind dream

Every child has a kind dream –
Chase it till it comes true.
However insurmountable things seem –
Allow the good seed to sprout through.

*Sunday*                    *23.04.2017*


# Be modest but smart

Be modest but smart,
It requires whole art.
One little thing for the start:
Smile, be brave with your loving heart!

*Sunday*                    *30.05.2010*

# When you believe in miracles

When you believe
In miracles – wonderful thing –
They happen and you receive.
Be sure to keep high your wing.

*Thursday*                                    *16.03.2017*


# Shine on

Keep calm and shine on!
It won't take long
Before hard things pass,
Before you figure out the mess!

*Saturday*                                    *26.03.2017*


# Share light

Shine your way –
Hard or light –
Have courage to say:
"You are so bright!"

But saying is insufficient –
Believe if you want all to be efficient.
Be of good cheer!
Share the things that are dear!

*Sunday*                                    *12.02.2017*

# Do not give up!

Do not give up!
That's what you need.
You're a winner –> that is your cup!
You love, you hope, you believe –
It's a diamond that's firm and not a broken reed!

*Saturday*                    *01.04.2006*


# If you are asking for a thing

If you are asking for a thing
And God does not give it to you –
Do not fold your wing –
He has prepared something better, something new.

*Thursday*                    *12.01.2017*


# Do good stuff today

In years to come
You will be more sorry about the things
You didn't do, because they would seem dumb,
Than about those you did on your faith, hope, love wings.

So do good stuff today,
Do it with courage, without delay.

Skip reflecting on what they will think or say –
Do kind, wise, and simple things at home, at work, at play.

*Wednesday*                              *28.12.2016*


# You are going to win

You are going to win,
Triumphant music will din.
I'm sure 'cause God is with you.
Your eye will enjoy the morning dew.

Believe 'cause you are strong,
Believe, love is never wrong.
Do not hesitate
And God will help at this rate.

*Saturday*                               *25.02.2006*


# Courage, patience, and smile

Courage, patience, and smile
Are the things to keep going –
Stock up to cover an extra mile,
Continue rowing.

*Sunday*                                 *11.09.2016*

# Keep on going (2)

When the things work wrong
And you want to despair, stop –
It won't take long
Before all is back to top.

Have courage, eat porridge;
Keep balance, use your talent –
Take it out of storage;
Be gallant.

*Sunday*                    *11.09.2016*


# God will make a way

God will make a way.
Believe as much as you can!
For the things you need – pray.
To give best things to you is His plan.

*Sunday*                    *07.08.2016*


# Whatever happens, keep on believing

Whatever happens, keep on believing.
Think, how much you can indeed,
You're as vigorous as a living seed.
Problems are nothing more than deceiving.

Whatever happens, believe.
Everything will be all right.
Be slow to quit, to leave,
You'll enjoy the sight.

Whatever happens, believe –
It's never too late to improve, to retrieve.
A race is won by racing,
A problem is solved by facing.

*Sunday*                              *24.09.2006*


# I'm not alone

Though all seems out of order,
And no one's willing to help,
I'm not alone on the border,
I am not going to yelp.

When no one seems to understand,
All the same I'm not alone.
No matter in air, at sea or on land,
I'll be strong as a stone.

Because God gives support.
What can be better in life?
Making me an invincible fort,
He crowns me with wisdom for strife.

*Saturday*                            *12.07.2008*

# How smart you are

How smart you are!
Believe, do not hesitate,
You'll be like a shining star,
You will enjoy success sooner or late!

With sun light your street will be lit,
He who has doubts is wrong.
Just do not cease doing your bit,
Indeed, you are strong!

*Sunday*                              *23.12.2007*


# Reveal your way to the Lord and be sincere

Reveal your way to the Lord and be sincere.
Hope in God and He will listen and attend to your need.
Trust in Him whether you go far or near.
Be courageous, take heed.

*June*                              *2016*

# Many are the afflictions of the righteous indeed

Many are the afflictions of the righteous indeed,
But God will deliver them from them all, in every need.

Sunday                          12.06.2016

# Be courageous in a lot of ways

Be courageous in a lot of ways.
Let your heart be strengthened,
All you who hope in the Lord all days.
Love Him for your years to be lengthened.

Be also harmless and smart;
God helps those who help themselves too.
Make wise and prompt your start.
Do your part, God will do His to help you break through.

*Sunday*                          *12.06.2016*

# When you believe
Miracles happen when you believe.
Just keep faith and continue going.
It's never too late to retrieve.
Keep trying and growing!
*Tuesday*                          *14.04.2015*

# Why are you upset

Why are you upset?
Every sunrise and every sunset
Bring hope.
Have courage, it's just a slope.

A rise will follow,
Keep on trying, dear fellow.
Keep your chin up and kind your heart.
Keep your head smart!

*Friday*                         *08.05.2015*


# Life is to improve

Life is to improve.
Look forward ahead!
It is okay to fall when you move.
No need to worry, be wiser instead.

*Thursday – Friday*              *24-25.03.2011*


# Have courage

When you act within the framework of the Commandments,
Do not be afraid to make a mistake.
Yes, in the future, you may need to make some amendments,
But any worthy enterprise you will be able to undertake.

Do not be sorry that you may miss a chance,
Neither in terms of money, nor in terms of a romance.
Focus on the main thing
And other things will follow:
To you your success will cling,
Your chest will not be hollow.

When it is hard, do not give up, keep on going.
Your success is in thinking and rowing.

*Sunday*                              *17.08.2014*


# Believe (3)

Believe in order to win!
Let your success be perfected.
Let your everyday life be affected!
Believe, be courageous and win.

Let God grant you faith.
Let your wisdom grow,
Let your love be in strength,
Let your life peacefully flow.

*Sunday*                              *17.07.2011*

# First

First do important things
Like family and work –
This will make abundant your fork;
Other things will hurry to succeed as if on wings.

*Saturday*                              *11.10.2014*

# We may get upset

We may get upset
Because something doesn't happen as we have set.
We tend to give up
Or to pretend it was not our tea cup.

We tend to forget when we get a lime
That all happens in God's time.
So, let's proceed with hope
That with His help we will achieve, we will cope!

*Wednesday*                              *10.02.2016*

# It's easy to give up

It's easy to give up
And not difficult to fall,
To stumble and to stop, to lose all.
But to go on, to make up…

It's not shameful to misfire,
But it's shameful not to get up.
Try, a bright ray will light up,
A clear dream will inspire.

*Saturday*                    *21.01.2006*


# Have faith to stand (2)

Have faith to stand.
Have faith, keep on going.
Whether you are plump or thin,
Continue building, not destroying!

*Monday – Saturday*              *09-21.12.2013*


# Have faith in God

If you want to win, fight a peaceful fight
For your and your children's future to be bright!
I know, this is hard,
But have faith in God and be en garde*!

Just a little more and the day of victory will come!
Be en garde, no need for rum,
Ahead, without despair, my friend!
You will enjoy victory in the end!

* French for "on guard".
*Sunday*                      *23.12.2012*

# You should never be afraid

You should never be afraid
God is always with you.
Be wise and do as He bade
And you will be given your due.

He cares even for the smallest flower.
Will He not care much more for you?
Remember His commandments and you will be stronger than
the highest tower.
It is never too late to improve, God loves you and that is true.

*Sunday*                                    *19.06.2005*


# Improve

It's never too late to improve,
Believe the Bible and try.
No one is to reprove.
With God you can achieve all though you are shy.

*Monday*                                    *16.03.2015*


# Every day is a new life

Every day is a new life
And we live, we say, and we run as if in a strife.

But there are things which are minor,
They will disappear on the horizon like a liner.

There are things which are essential,
They must be treated in a way which is differential.
Minor matters draw to the earth and lower in fact;
Essential things require patience and tact.

What's the difference you say?
Watch and you will see as clear as day:
The award for the minor things is none,
The award for essential ones is blessing with every new dawn.

*Sunday*                              *14.10.2007*


# Shine your way

Shine your way,
Do good things whatever they say!
Have salt in yourself and have light,
Make your chemin* bright!

Rely on God and go!
In terms of helping people are slow.
You are beautiful, strong, and smart.
With God's help you will achieve all, just do your part!

* French for "way".

*Monday*                              *22.12.2014*

# Your strength is in rowing

When there seems to be no escape,
Keep on going.
If something does not stick, use a tape.
Your strength is in rowing.

*Friday*                              *26.09.2014*


# I admire you

The only thing I want you to remember
After reading these lines:
You are awesome January through December!

You are worthy whatever they say/think
And I want you to stay healthy whether you like vegies or meat,
grey colour or pink.

You are valuable, much more than gold.
Inside of you there is a chest of treasures the key to which you
hold.

You are precious in God's sight:
Your every hair is counted.
I admire you: your heart is pure and brave, your head is so
bright!

*Sunday*                              *16.08.2015*

# Whatever happens, believe

It is easy to believe when all is smooth,
But try to be consistent whatsoever:
No matter who would like you to lose,
God is with you forever.

Whatever happens, believe.
Let your heart follow your dream.
Whatever news you receive,
Let your soul faithfully gleam!

*Saturday*                    *05.02.2011*


# Rely on God with Him you will show strength

Rely on God; with Him, you will show strength.
With Him, you will extend your days' length.
You will conquer any foe,
You will mix the tastiest dough.

Rely on God and win with peace in any land.
Take a shield of faith in hand
And a spear of love, and an armour of hope
To manage all and to be able to cope.

*Wednesday*                    *06.05.2015*

# Your kind dream

Believe and follow your dream –
You have the aim to achieve.
However hard it will seem,
Do not get discouraged; believe!

*Monday*                    *23.08.2010*


# Give me just a little smile

Give me just a little smile,
You have your own beautiful style.
Whatever it is, it will soon pass.
Cheer up, look at the greenness of grass.

You have an amazing head;
Not relying on force, you use it instead.
You are beautiful and strong in your way!
Be wise and harmless whatever they say!

*Saturday*                    *23.05.2015*


# Do not get upset

If you can't catch anything with your rod,
Don't worry, you'll soon catch a cod;

If you have nothing to dine,
It's ok, you'll get slimmer, it'll be fine.

Have you sat on some orange?
Never mind, someone sat on porridge.

Never get upset,
Your problems can be easily set!

*Friday*                    *19.11.2004*


# He will not suffer your foot to be moved

He will not suffer your foot to be moved,
He will help all your affairs get improved.
God That keeps you will not slumber.
He multiplies your posterity without number.

The sun will not smite you by day, nor the moon by night.
He sends success, peace, and might.
Glory to God now and forever!
Live your faith and be clever!

*Tuesday*                    *09.06.2015*


# The Lord is on my side, I will not fear

The Lord is on my side, I will not fear.
What can man do to me? I will run to the aim as a deer.

213

I will not step back or hesitate.
I will run, I will read, I will be in a healthy state.

*Tuesday*                    *02.06.2015*


# Cheer up

Do your part,
God will do His, be sure.
Do things with faith and hope in heart;
Let love not depart.

Do your part,
God will do His, truly.
Add kindness and confidence to start;
Thrive fully.

*Tuesday*                    *21.04.2015*


# Keep on going (3)

Keep on going, do not give up the fight.
Let your mind be clever, let your feet be light!
Let you face shine, let people around delight!
Pray and continue being bright!

*Saturday*                    *23.05.2015*

# LET US CELEBRATE

# TOGETHER

## Christmas Joy

Today the Great Joy came;
Therefore, let no one be sad:
Wise and silly, fit and lame,
Rich and poor, single and Dad.

The Peace has come;
Let no one be thinking of rage;
Let all be armed with love at least with some;
Let us sing, let us be sage.

This Day the King of unity
Has joined forces with us,
Therefore, our focus is the community;
Let us rejoice, seek peace and share the Christmas spirit thus.

*Sunday*                                    *23.12.2018*


## Here we are

Here we are,
One more year has passed.
People are brothers, they are not far;
Bad luck will end – it won't last.

What have we managed to do?
Did we cope?
We could have much better, it's true.
Let's try and next year will bring much success. I hope.

What one needs is being sage,
And we'll arrange our time.
We'll avoid everyday's vanity cage.
Who believes in God will enjoy the real prime!

*Sunday*                                   *30.12.2007*


# When Pascha comes – rejoice

When Pascha comes – rejoice:
Those who have fasted and those who have not; –
Let the joy be in your heart and voice –
In the Kingdom, there are different chambers and there are a lot
–

Those who have come early and those who have come late;
Those who push forward and those who contemplate –
Let all share the joy –
Let all accept it as children, a girl and a boy!

*Thursday*                                 *21.03.2018*

# Thank You Father for this year too!

Thank You Father for this year too!
How interesting life is!
And this year is so pure and new.
You take care of all: people, birds, bees...

New Year has come,
What a wonderful night!
The clock has stricken 12-time "bum".
Christmas lights are shining so bright!

I wish you a happy New Year!
It has rushed in
Bringing in fresh hope and faithful glare!
Rely on God and keep up your chin!

*Monday*                    *01.01.2007*


# Open your heart for Christmas

Christmas, what a bright Day!
It's time to smile, give, take, and pray!
It's time when you can play
As if you were a child constructing with clay.

Open your heart, let Christmas come and stay,
Let the kind child in you rejoice at each sun ray!
Keep your own bright, courageous, perseverant way.
Merry Christmas! I wish you happy smiles and a full tray!
*Sunday*                    *24.12.2017*

# Christmas presents

Do presents on Christmas matter?
Yes, they certainly do!
Not the ones that make us fatter,
But the ones that melt hearts and show our love to be true.

The ones that unite our hearts,
The ones that make distance short,
The ones that extinguish burning darts.
Faith, hope, love; the ones that comfort.

Friendly smile,
Cheering wink,
Prayer, charity, kind deed that lasts a while,
Peaceful mind... Have time to stop and think.

*Wednesday*                    *20.12.2017*


# Bells are singing a merry tune

Bells are singing a merry tune
Above the city and country, forest, and dune;
The Wonderful Day is coming here,
Fairy Christmas is already near.

Don't hesitate,
Open your heart till it's not too late:
All your dreams will come true,
Believe and the rain of grace will pour upon you.

You are free in God, so –
More confidence, be ready to mow.
Merry Christmas I wish!
Be blessed and enjoy your Christmas dish!

*Tuesday 20.12.2005 – Saturday 28.01.2006*

# Christmas is coming

Bells are singing,
Wonderful tunes are ringing!
Smile, blessed you are!
Let your heart follow Jesus, our Star!

Christmas is coming, listen and look!
Everyone is going carol-singing, even a rook.
Give your neighbour a smile!
Be yourself, show your kind heart, your own style!

*Saturday*                              *31.12.2005*

# New Year (1)

Another year is slipping away,
It's useless to ask it to stay.
What is done cannot be undone;
Time is flying, the moment is gone.

But who said
That nothing can be done instead?
A New Year is a new hope,
You'll manage, you'll cope!

Spread your wings;
How many fruits the good brings!
It's Christmastide,
Let love inside!

*Saturday*                    *31.12.2005*


# Peace

Love peace and cling to it,
But be ready that some may search for war.
This desire of theirs is a pit.
They will lose, they won't even get a draw.

Pray for yourself, your family, and neighbour,
Pray for love and peace, but be ready
That some may despise your labour.
In all trust in God Who makes us steady.

And let your Christian banner float, whether you work or dine.
Let your simple light shine!
Have salt in yourself and have love.
You long for peace and you will see the peace dove.

*Tuesday*                    *17.02.2015*

# Oh come, let us worship and bow down before Christ

Oh come, let us worship and bow down
Before Christ our God, let us sing psalms!
Come, let us rejoice in village and in town!
Let us give alms!

Let no one be upset.
It is Easter, the Feast of feasts, the greatest Day!
It is time to forgive any debt,
It is time to soften our hearts and to pray.

*Friday*                                    *10.04.2015*


# Happy New Year

Happy New Year!
Please, remain always kind and fair.
Do not be shy to display your smile,
Show your own friendly style!

The coming year will be like a toy,
It'll bring you health, happiness, joy!
Comb your beautiful hair,
Happy New Year!

# Let Christmas light up souls

Let Christmas light up souls,
It's time for a merry song!
All people are together just having their own roles.
Love will last forever and more and it isn't long.

So, smile and join your hands
Forgive all you couldn't before.
Your heart is longing to see new kind lands,
How much good your soul does store!

Christmas is coming,
What a bright Day!
Children are joyfully running,
All can come true for those who hopefully pray!

'Merry Christmas!', we say
And it is indeed!
On God our hopes we lay,
So, why to worry, there is no need!

*Sunday*                     *24.12.2006*


# Christmas bells are singing,

Christmas bells are singing,
How blissfully calm is their ringing!
It's a song of life for all,
Let's open our hearts to a poor man's call!

Never close your soul and it'll be cured.
Hardships are given to be sagely endured.
However difficult sometimes it may be,
You are born to win, not to flee!

*Saturday – Sunday*                    *15-16.12.2007*

# The Feast of Feasts

The Feast of Pascha has passed,
But the joy and victory of life last.
Let your heart remember this fact;
Let your smile and good deeds correspondingly act.

*Bright Monday*              *02.05.2016*

# On Easter

Easter! What a fine day!
No one's gloom will stay.
Today no place for fear!

Life has won!
Today forget problems, have fun.
Thank Thee Father for all!
Thou saved us from a terrible fall.

Hallowed be Your Name!
Thou crown people with fame.

Easter! And life rejoices forever!
Thou make us happy and clever.

*Saturday*                    *18.04.2016*


# Easter

Easter is knocking at doors.
What a wonderful day!
We can open hearts' stores!
It's a day of love, of the hopeful ray!

Death will always lose.
It will never own.
Let a winning hymn make a cruise!
How high our song has flown!

Our prayers are heard!
You are not alone.
God takes care even of a bird!
Smile! Believe, you won't knock against a stone.

*Saturday – Monday*              *22-24.04.2006*


# It's Christmas today

It's Christmas today,
The time when miracles take place.

It's time to do good things and to play.
All is rejoicing: the earth and space!

Come out, sing carols, cheerful songs
To your family and friend
Or a soul that awaits Christmas and longs.
Glorify God, let Christmas in heart never end!

*Tuesday*                     *06.01.2015*

# The first carol

Did you know that the first carol ever
Was sung by angels and shepherds heard?
They left all to come, but brought their herd.
Magi came too: their decision was clever.

Let us set aside all cares of life –
Let's come to Church to celebrate Christmas together!
Be your kind self, bring your friends, your children, and wife.
Set aside worries, today be lighter than a feather!

*Tuesday – Wednesday*             *29-30.12.2015*

# Without Christmas, there is no Easter

Without Christmas, there is no Easter;
Life, salvation, and joy from both these events proceed.

Therefore, take heed:
Rejoice in both feasts and help those who are in need.

During Christmas, however, there is a risk of greed
Over presents such as a toy, a sweater, a golden bead;
But open your heart and open the Bible to read –
Let God take the lead!

*Monday – Tuesday*                    *28-29.12.2015*


# This is the greatest day of the year

This is the Greatest Day of the year
It's time for the Christmas song!
And I wish you a Merry Christmas and a Happy New Year!
Some days seemed to be so long…

But Christmas is quite different.
You've been looking forward to this night.
Today forget about the rent,
Everything will be all right.

*Saturday*                    *20.12.2003*


# Share the Christmas Spirit

A good way to share the Christmas Spirit is to sing together,
To make people's mood lighter than a feather!

So, come, join the song,
Don't be afraid to be wrong.

Let's sing about His glory and love!
Let's ask for a peace dove
For all the people, near and far!
Let's wait and watch the first star.

It's Christmas, do sing and believe!
You will receive
The things you need.
The reward is great for every kind deed.

God loves you very much;
The extent of this love is such
That He gave His Only-begotten Son for you.
He wants you to be happy and to break through.

*Sunday*                    *20.12.2015*


# Carol

Today is Christmas, let's sing with cheer.
Christ is born to save us all.
Let us give up fear!
Today our salvation and joy are near.

Let us stock up with love
To the Lord and our neighbour!
Let us give to those in need a glove,
Yet better a pair for God blessed us in our labour!

Let us sing with joy
And let us share
A kind word, a toque, organic food, a toy…
Let us enjoy Christmas glare!

*Tuesday – Thursday*          *16-18.12.2014*


# Christmas carol

It's Christmas season outside,
It's time to let the Christmas Spirit inside.
It's time to help him/her who is in need,
To invite the Christmas Spirit through a kind deed.

It's time to find peace with all,
To open your own heart, to go beyond a mall;
To phone him/her who needs your call;
To speak to the one who is in low spirits over a fall.

It's time to believe in miracles, friend;
For him who does, they never end.
Christmas is time to be a good Christian, husband, and son,
To spend time with your family and to have fun!

*Thursday*          *10.12.2015*

# New Year (2)

Let this New Year
Be for all people fair;
Let people's love grow
So that we all learned to appreciate, to support, to bestow! =)

*Saturday*                              *31.12.2011*

# MISCELLANEOUS

## In God we shall work power

In God we shall work power!
He crowns us with beauty more than that of a flower!
He helps us to score the goal!
He replenishes our bowl.

*Sunday*                                        *17.07.2016*


## Some people are eager to earn

Some people are eager to earn,
But it does them an ill turn.
I wish they could see
The real fruits of the real tree…

Gold gives power, they think;
They forgot it can bend to its will in a wink.
It's impossible to serve mammon and to be happy,
It's impossible to decay and to be snappy.

I don't say go poor,
Just let your soul be pure.
Love will make your days sunny,
Life is not all money.

*Monday – Tuesday*                          *19-20.12.2005*

# When we do not speak

When we do not speak,
We may hear so much!
No matter whether you are strong or weak,
A Brazilian or a Dutch.

*March*                    *2012*


# Orthodox preacher

The less you speak, write or post,
The more they listen and read.
Communicate clearly and what's needed the most.
Be brief, do not overfeed.

*Sunday*                    *26.11.2017*


# If you want a change

If you want a change,
Begin from yourself.
There is a wide range,
Add up a pinch of wiliness from the shelf.

If you want politeness,
Then why are you rude?
You say, not enough rightness?
How much have you done?... to conclude.

It is pretty simple,
You crop what you sow.
When you smile, you have a dimple,
You reach only when you go.

If you need respect, respect;
If you want love, be generous with it.
You will see people react.
But be hasty, days do fleet.

*Monday*                    *09.02.2009*


# Nerve bumps

There are speed bumps on roads:
They prevent from speeding, especially cars with loads.
Have you thought of nerve bumps ever?
We need to set those in our minds to avoid worrying and to be
clever.

*Monday*                    *22.07.2018*


# Oh Lord, forgive me for being slow

Oh Lord, forgive me for being slow…
Teach me in Your faith and love to grow,
To be in time for Your service and prayer,
To be kind, wise, and fair!
*Sunday*                    *10.06.2012*

# Volleyball

Volleyball is a game for the agile.
It trains your reaction and wit.
It is for the young and the senior; for the strong and the fragile.
Using it for fun and health is a good tip.

It doesn't tire you out,
But you sleep well and become stout.
It expands your circle of friends.
To good mood it lends!

*Thursday – Sunday*                    *13-16.09.2018*


# Listen

Listen to others,
If to be listened you want.
Listen to your sisters and brothers;
Their knowledge will be your reward.

You think that you are smart,
That's all right,
But listening is the start
Bringing your intellect into sight!

*Thursday*                    *21.10.2018*

# Icons

We are not praying to icons at all.
We are praying with icons on a wall.
Like the Book*, icons help tell the story;
They remind what we've read to God's glory.

*The Bible.

*Sunday*                                        *15.04.2018*


# Fasting is not a sad time

Fasting is not a sad time –
It is a time for improvement,
When out of sleep you get into movement,
Out of a spiritual winter right into a prime.

Use it wisely, with joy,
To build confidence, success;
To help move ahead for less.
Thank, achieve, enjoy.

*Wednesday*                                    *18.07.2018*


# When people look at you

When people look at you,
Make them want to live:

Look and be positive, say "HRU".
You have a good mood to share, high spirits to give.

*Friday*                          *15.06.2018*

# Live so that you're sure

Live so that you're sure
That tomorrow you will not be sorry.
To do kind deeds we are mature;
Open your heart, you need no worry.

*Tuesday*                          *03.03.2009*

# Veggies, prayers, courage

Eat your veggies!
Say your prayers!
Smoothen quarrel edges.
Stock up with courage; eliminate worry on all levels.

*Thursday*                          *31.05.2018*

# A sea needs streams in order not to dry out

A sea needs streams in order not to dry out;
Earth needs water to grow seeds.
A body needs food to be stout;
And a soul is in need of good deeds.

*Sunday*                              *29.10.2006*

# The Church is not a building

The Church is not a building –
It is people like you and me
Who come to pray without yielding
To everyday's hassle, who are prejudice-free.

*Sunday*                              *23.04.2017*

# He always felt so frustrated

He always felt so frustrated
Being underestimated, that's true.
Really, their opinions were dated.
He did his best to break through.

But as the years went on,
He grew older.

Everything has changed: rich watch, bored yawn;
Unhappy and harsh comments, eyes that are colder...

Yesterday he fired two of his men,
He said, "They laze".

Both are wrong: those who did not appreciate him then
And he because he forgot and grew chary of praise.

*Saturday*                    *19.11.2005*


# When you're ill

When you're ill,
It's time to change,
To jump over the hill,
To switch to a better range.

Think what you can do.
You can improve the things,
Believe, it's true.
You can readjust your strings.

So, it's time;
Keep your heart pure and your vision – clear.
Sour is a lime,
And your deeds are dear.

*Tuesday*                    *05.05.2009*

# Orthodox and smart

Orthodox people must be smart.
Smart thing #1 – love God in all,
Let this be fully, not in part.
Smart thing #2 – love your neighbour at home and in a mall.

Also be smart in work and studies;
Be smart in eating, drinking, speaking;
Be smart with your lady, friends, buddies;
Be smart in completing good projects through, avoiding
freaking.

*Thursday*                              *21.07.2016*


# What matters most

When we are in extreme situations,
It's what seems the least that matters the most:
Prayer, a word of support, and patience,
Faith, hope, love a quarrel closed,

Repentance, Communion, communication,
Fresh air, sleep, enough water and rest.
Therefore, remember these at all times, in any nation.
In loving God and neighbour – do your best.

*Sunday*                                *11.03.2018*

# Time passes fast

Time passes fast:
You are eighteen, you nap,
And you are forty and the younger years are in the past.
Do all good, kind, courageous stuff now – to recap.

*Sunday*                                    *18.06.2017*


# Don't be sorry

Don't be sorry and you won't be sorry!
You must learn to give up worry.
In whatever things you need, repent,
You can always use a prayer and Lent.

Repentance means fixing whatever you can
While also putting worries to ban.
Repent and let God light up your heart.
Repentance is turning around and having new start.

*Saturday*                                  *07.07.2017*


# The right choice

The right choices aren't always easy,
But they aren't always hard.
Take prayer, for instance, when you are free or busy,
It protects from being caught off guard.

Use it in the morning, at night
And as often as needed.
Let your soul be light,
Let good stuff in your heart be seeded.

Prayer "takes away" minutes, but saves days;
It promotes health and cheer;
It opens new ways;
It directs to God and all things that are dear.

*Wednesday*                    *14.02.2018*


# If you feel down

If you feel down
Without a reason,
Don't worry, don't frown –
This happens to me and all in any season.

Fresh air, good sleep, and food;
Family, friends, communication
Are the things that help do good.
Prayer and hope are a must in this equation.

*Friday*                    *19.05.2017*

# Baptism

Did you know
That in Baptism indeed
We are baptized in Christ's death?
For sin we are dead, in Christ we live and glow;
We give ourselves to Him to lead
From the beginning till the last breath.

*Thursday*                    *27.04.2017*


# How rich we are

How rich we are;
How happy we could be;
Our friendship could be as a sparkling star.
Why do we refuse to see?

We have legs and hands, ears and eyes as well...
Isn't it enough to form a world-wide community;
Isn't it enough to help those who fell?
Power is in our unity.

All the world's gold
Isn't worth a child's wound or cry.
Peace! How many times we were told!
But tomorrow may be too late to try.

*Saturday*                    *23.04.2005*

# Do things at once

Do things at once
Like helping the poor,
Like completing a task.
Be the doer,
Praise, give, ask.
Always in prayer,
Patient, but never an idle "stayer".

*Friday*                    *20.10.2017*


# Help us

Gracious Father, help
As You always did.
We are in trouble and yelp,
Save and cure, we'll do, just say, just bid.

*Tuesday*               *20.12.2005*


# Travels make me wise and stronger

Travels make me wise and stronger
So that I could stand longer.
And what I missed at school,
I will learn, it's like a rule.

New people, communication,
Good friends, fresh information,
I'll learn and see much new;
It's like a breeze, like morning dew.

*Friday*                    *01.08.2008*


# Why trying to be kind if I'm silly

Why trying to be kind if I'm silly?
And all my ways are hilly...
I want to help, but often do worse indeed.
What shall I do? What do I need?

I know, the answer's not far,
But how it's difficult to see the right star.
Father, help me, please.
I do need wisdom, only Thou can give the keys.

*Sunday*                    *27.08.2006*


# All that we do should be nice

All that we do should be nice:
Helping others, working, studying, eating rice.
Let others see and want to imitate,
But let us be true and practice what we state.

*Sunday*                    *08.09.2013*

# Your hands do what's on your heart

Think about good
And this will help.
It will change not only your mood,
But your life, you'll never yelp.

Still don't believe?
Try, of course, if you can…
Why would I deceive?
Let peaceful mind build your plan.

*Saturday*                    *07.01.2006*


# Love blessing and use your wit

Love God and seek blessing
And it will cling to you.
If you do something wrong, be swift on confessing:
We all need to renew,

There is no shame in it.
Love peace and it will come to you.
To make progress use your wit.
Oh, how much it is true!

*Sunday*                    *2014*

# It's easy to lose

It's easy to lose,
But it's difficult to find.
Today you're on the booze,
But tomorrow, be sure, the fortune won't be so kind.

You say you weren't ready?
I say you didn't want to
'Cause you knew you had to be strong and steady.
You'll have to be wise to break through.

*Saturday*                    *22.05.2004*


# If we are ready to strive

If we are ready to strive,
We must not doubt at all.
You are strong and sage, you are alive –
You are born to win, not to fall!

*Sunday*                    *30.12.2007*


# What is going on around?

What is going on around?
Life is rushing by.
I can hear its sound,
It's like being in a field of rye.

246

I live and discover,
I've been wrong about so many things.
But God always helps me to recover
Giving me hope and invisible wings.

I don't know
What will happen in a day:
Perhaps it'll be sunny, perhaps, it will snow.
How important it is to be sure on the way!

*Monday –Tuesday*                    *18-19.12.2006*


# Some moments you want to pass fast

Some moments you want to pass fast.
Black stripe, white stripe…
Some moments you do want to last,
But wait, do not wipe.

All sorts of things make up our life.
In all, it is so good
With every smile, every strife.
It is worth living I can conclude.

Be sorry about nothing:
One moment and the present is the past.
There is no use fussing.
Always ahead, your world is vast!

*Saturday*                    *01.11.2008*

# Upon God I will rely

Incredible, how changes are fast!
Man proposes,
But God disposes.
It's all true to the last!

No use relying on men...
You'll pay a double price,
But won't get a bit of your rice.
What shall I do then?

Upon God I will rely!
Being patient and sage,
Quick at learning, slow at rage,
Always in action, never too shy!

*Saturday*                    *28.06.2008*


# You're not alone, believe

You're not alone, believe,
God is always with you!
Cheer up, it's too early to leave,
You are right, you're strong, it's true!

Find your niche and go on;
Persistent thou should be,
And you'll still admire the dawn
Enjoying the daylight brighter than you thought it could be.

We are together,
You are not alone.
Even in a rainy weather
God's love will bring us together making stronger than a stone.

*Saturday*                    *27.10.2007*


# Be friend to God

Be slave to God and not to men.
Fear God on all your ways.
Be not afraid of people now or then.
May God prolong your days!

May they be filled with health and joy!
Fear God and not men to achieve your goal:
You have a smart head, employ!
Keep straight your back and sound your soul!

*October*                    *2014*


# Seek the Lord and His strength always

Seek the Lord and His strength always –
This will prolong the length of your days
And will fill them with joy.
Health and respect you will enjoy!

*Wednesday*                    *22.04.2015*

# Coming to Church

No need knocking
When you come to Church.
No need self-locking;
No need knocking on birch.

Be yourself, say prayer,
Be sincere;
Keep fair;
Abandon fear.

*Saturday*                    *13.05.2017*


# When do you live?

There is no tomorrow,
No yesterday as well.
Save now in order not to borrow;
Listen to the ringing bell.

Life is signing now.
Putting off a kind deed
Is to pinch your own brow,
It is to refuse an essential need.

By doing good to a neighbour
You do good to yourself first of all.
Good deed for soul is daily bread and labour.
Say "today" in order not to fall.
*Monday*                    *09.02.2009*

# Lord, bless

Let them curse, but You, o Lord, bless.
With Your blessing I can achieve –
They want more, but get less –
God, teach us all to believe.

*Saturday*                    *23.05.2015*


# The Church

The Church is a member of my family truly –
It helps bring up children duly.
For many things I am obliged to the Church indeed –
It taught love; from vices it freed.

*Thursday*                    *20.04.2017*


# When you can, give

When you can, give.
And you will be given.
Be gracious and thankful and live,
You never know where you will be driven.

What you have, do not hide,
Open your mind, be bright.
Let your life outlook be wide;
Keep your inner spark always in sight!
*Thursday*                    *06.11.2008*

# You know better than I

God, let me remember
That You know better than I,
January through December:
When I pray, when I say, and when I cry.

Continue spreading Your grace
Without which Your slave
Would have worst things to face:
Illness, poverty, failure, grave.

You know better than I.
Let it be so
Whether I stand or lie
Let Your slave prosper in You and with You let him grow.

*Saturday*                      *01.04.2017*


# When I save on fruits

When I save on fruits,
I spend on doctors more.
Look at both, the top and the roots,
The outer part and the core.
*Thursday*                  *16.03.2017*

# How wrong I was

How wrong I was.
All my problems come from within.
But now I see better the cause,
And the struggle is the way to win.

I thought that I had no luck.
Then I saw a disabled child
And realized where I got stuck.
I had all and was sad – in contrast, he smiled.

I say enough,
It's never too late to mend!
My heart must be no longer rough
'Cause God's grace has no end.

So, should I complain
Or be ungrateful for a while?
Never! Isn't it plain?
Thank Thee, Father, for the child's smile!

*Sunday*                              *15.04.2007*


# If God has pronounced against a nation

If God has pronounced against a nation,
But these people repent:
God will spare this population;
To them, an angel of peace and health will be sent.

If God's people, who are elect,
Have gone astray,
God will see and detect:
He will punish unless they go back to the righteous way.

*Pascha Sunday*                    *12.04.2015*


# Be your kind self

One hundred years
Pass faster than you think,
But don't worry, open your ears;
Say "thank you", give a wink!

*Sunday*                              *19.02.2017*


# This could be a song

Open your heart.
That's exactly what you need.
And let us be smart.
Sharpen your soul's trusty reed –
Open your heart.

Just let some love inside
And it will live and succeed
Flowering with happiness by side.
It'll be your shield in court, it'll plead.

Love does not beg, but gives;
Has noting, but is rich;
A real love never dies, but lives.
Love is the treasure available for each.

*Saturday*                    *18.02.2006*


# Avoid war by all means

Avoid war by all means;
In it no one wins.
Shame is on those who unleash wars,
Who lie and break laws.

Repent and seek peace
Or vanish with all yours to the last piece.
Pray, may God help you find the way.
Believe there is a chance for you whatever they say.

*Sunday*                    *14.09.2014*


# Dressed up for weather
Do not be shy of dressing up for the weather.
Do not consider too much what people will think:
They will admire! Whether
You realize this or not. Appropriate clothes are a link
To healthy you. Who needs young people who are sick?
Before going out, search the weather, make that extra click!
*Sunday*                    *01.02.2015*

# Crosses of others

None of us knows
The crosses of others;
Therefore, wherever each of us goes
Let us be patient with sisters and brothers.

*Thursday*                              *02.02.2017*


# Exercises will help you stay well

Exercises will help you stay well:
Your body will sound as a new, tuned bell;
Your eyes will see as eagle eyes;
Your brain will work to make you wise.

Choose exercises that fit your style:
Swimming, running, stretching, walking a mile…
In the morning or in the eve.
Then, a healthy soul in a healthy body is what you will receive!

*Sunday*                              *03.02.2013*


# Love justice and walk humbly with the Lord

Love justice in every business, in all,
And be prepared to walk humbly with the Lord.

He is the One Who hears and listens to your call.
Rely on Him, His deeds, His Word.

*Monday*                    *03.10.2016*


# What is my destination?

What is my destination?
That's the question I should ask.
Have I mistaken my vocation?
Will I be able to solve the task?

I just live my short life
Trying to hope for the best,
It's like a strife
And I should work with zest.

All the above is right,
But sometimes I feel wrong,
Now I know my belief should be bright
And also hope and love; and they all life-long.

*Saturday*                    *11.12.2004*


# When you hear crying,

When you hear crying,
Do not shut your ears, explore
Whether this is a call for help or lying;

257

Act according to the situation: use a word of support, buy food in a store.

*Monday*                    *05.09.2016*


# No, I won't stop

No, I won't stop.
I will go on till I reach the end!
By slow rowing and a quick hop,
I will graduate as I intend!

*Sunday*                    *20.11.2016*


# Try everything

When you are too afraid to go,
Try everything – all worthy things to grow.
When you are ready to quit,
Just try your wit.

In all good business keep smart and fair;
Before you make an important decision, remember to say a prayer.
Be simple and clever,
Be grateful ever.

*Sunday*                    *20.11.2016*

# A beautiful smile

You have a beautiful smile
Which can help cover a mile,
Cope with a difficult file –
Smile often, it is worthwhile.

*Tuesday*                    *15.11.2016*


# You're at the fire-place

You're at the fire-place
And do not feel cold,
And you've got some stores just in case,
But don't be bold.

Everything is in God's power.
Do you remember paupers near your house?
They aren't afraid of showers,
They believe though they've got as much as a mouse.

All you have is like a passing dream;
Even some paupers used to be rich.
Life is faster than a mountain stream –
While you can, help those who can't do a hitch.

*Saturday*                    *04.12.2004*

# Everything positive

Every year has Christmas cheer;
Every month has a pay day;
Every week has a day-off gear;
Every day has a morning ray...

*Sunday*                                    *09.10.2016*


# If you want to be sage

If you want to be sage,
Be patient, forget about rage.
Learn to listen first of all
And you will stand where talkative people fall.

And then don't be shy to ask;
Good advice is a half done task.
Don't be too fast to act.
On time though you should react.

Wisdom is close,
He who accepts it will thrive like a rose.
Wisdom is calling for you.
So, listen to get your due.

*Sunday*                                    *23.09.2007*

# Even blind person can see while believes

You went bust
And tried to drown the misfortune in whisky.
Your mind dimmed and liver suffered rust.
Became better? No! More risky!

Have you lost your hand
Like the guy?
Or your eyesight? So tell me why,
Why can't you see the rich land?

Even those poor guys
Do not look back closing their eyes.
A deaf man will see the rise,
A blind man will hear it 'cause he tries.

Enough, stand up, just start.
Think about your heart
Which you can't deceive.
You've got to believe.

*Saturday*                    *04.02.2006*


# Keep up with the time

Keep up with the time,
Be smart in the things you do.
Be faithful however high you climb.
Let your love, your health, your words be true.
*Monday*                    *05.09.2016*

# Do not be afraid to bestow

Do not be afraid to bestow,
What you give, you get back,
The miser's pocket cannot bestow,
But a kind heart will never lack.

Never take pride,
Only God knows what's ahead;
The good is on your side;
Don't be proud, better wise instead.

Do not be shy to help
'Cause life is like a running stream,
I hope you'll never yelp
And never be deaf to a scream.

*Friday*                            *26.11.2004*


# He left his home so long ago

He left his home so long ago,
They were telling him, "You're cool!",
But soon he had nowhere to stay or go.
Well, he wasn't a fool.

The man had relied on money
And not on wisdom's voice;
The money flew away like fresh honey,
But it was his own way, his own choice.

His cash disappeared
And so did his jolly friends,
But the young man wasn't yet feared,
He just realized that a road often bends.

Now his bedroom was a park,
His dreams were his food;
He went to sleep with dogs' bark,
Try to imagine his mood.

But it's time for me to end.
The young man came home.
Wisdom became his new friend,
Clouds never appeared above his dome.

His experience wasn't funny,
But he realized that it's never too late to improve
And it's useless to rely on money.
Well, I've tried to retell the story, but haven't meant to prove.

*Saturday*                    *16.04.2005*


# Tweet true things

Tweet true things
And let your tweets be kind!
Let your tweets help spread wings.
Let them be seasoned with humour to cheer mind!

*Sunday*                    *25.11.2012*

# Do kind things

Do kind things
And do not wait for thanks.
Spread your gorgeous wings!
You are strong without ranks.

Let you colours shine,
Let your smile cure!
Follow the kind line,
Let your body and soul be pure.

*Sunday*                                    *03.05.2010*


# Good fasting

Fasting can and should be for pleasure –
Even with fasting we need to know measure.
Fasting that is unhealthy
Is not pleasing to God, be it a poor man or wealthy.

Let your fasting be good for body and soul;
Let it help you achieve your spiritual goal;
Let it be helpful for charity and prayer;
Let it help you become a better Christian on every layer.

*Thursday*                                  *05.05.2016*

# Vain is the help of man

Vain is the help of man.
Through God we will show strength.
It is useless to rely on what man can.
If you want to enjoy victories at length,

Rely on God in all.
He beautifies your head with a crown;
He protects from a fall;
He dresses you with a PhD gown!

*Tuesday*                    *12.05.2015*


# Saints among us

Have you ever thought
That there are saints among us?
In the street, in Church, at school, at work, on a bus?
Maybe, when you forgot

To lock your car,
They were there for you.
They went the way all the way through.
They cared whether you were close or far.

They looked after your baby.
They fed your dog.
They protected against a rogue.
They did not read your mind, maybe,

But they prayed for you every day.
I know, somebody hurt us in the past –
Now for seeing good stuff we are not fast,
But let's keep our hearts open June through May.

*Monday*                    *18.04.2016*


## Nonverbal

We like to see.
"Seeing is believing"
The proverb says to thee,
What nonverbals are we receiving?

Be smart to gesture
And kind to smile.
That's a good communication texture,
Watch people for a while.

*Friday*                    *21.05.2010*


## There is no unforgiven sin

There is no unforgiven sin –
There is only an unrepented one.
Repent to lighten your heart and to win:
Be wise and harmless, read and run.

*Saturday*                    *02.04.2016*

# What you do is important

What you do is important really:
Your job, your studies, your family, and your sport;
The things for which you get paid and the ones you give freely.
Your kind deeds are your fort.

Every kind deed matters.
Not because of the one who flatters,
But because they improve the world around,
Because they evoke a smile and make happiness abound.

Never question a kind deed you do,
Stay faithful to what is true.
Good intentions may mislead.
So, keep it simple when you do your duty and a kind deed.

Be sure to fulfill your duty in work and studies.
Train to respect your time your party buddies.
Live simple life of faith every day.
Keep it simple and pray.

*Monday*                    *04.04.2016*


# Rely on God at large

Rely on God at large:
Your worries will disappear like a retiring barge;
Your weaknesses at length
Will change to strength!
*Sunday*                    *30.10.2011*

# Why is Church important

When you go to Church, you are its part.
Go to Church in simplicity of heart –
Not because somebody tells you,
But because you love, because your faith is true.

*Monday*                    *21.03.2016*


# Remain humble and kind

In any situation remain humble and kind,
Among any nation, whether you reach high or fall behind –
Remain humble and kind in all;
Let your attitude build bridges, not a wall.

*Monday*                    *29.02.2016*


# Air, exercises, water, and sleep

Fresh air, physical + thinking exercises, and water
Are some of the things that help maintain health and stay sharp.
These things are good for you, your wife, your son and
daughter.
Implement to feel like fish in water, like a carp.

Another thing is sufficient sleep.
Use it to stay active during the day,

To be able to think in a way which is deep,
To have strength to prepare more hay.

*Saturday*                    *20.02.2016*

# Eat organic food

Eat organic food –
For health it is good.
Our body is an organism:
Improvement in one thing triggers
Improvement in other things like a mechanism.

*Saturday*                    *20.02.2016*

# When you feel right, smile

When you feel right, smile,
Show your own free style.
Do not restrain your mood –
Your heart is kind, you look so good.

Only God knows what will happen tomorrow.
Happiness may change to sorrow.
But this is not the reason for crying,
You'd better keep trying!

You will have much success, I am sure,
You do have a chance to change the score.

Be yourself, no matter where you are;
God's support is here, not far.

*Tuesday – Sunday*                    *04-16.12.2007*

# Wisdom begins with the fear of God

Wisdom begins with the fear of God indeed:
It will help you in studies, work, and every need.

But what does it mean to fear God in the right way?
To cease from doing and freeze? No, but to work hard and to
pray.

The fear of the Lord shows itself in doing:
In loving God and with His commandments continuing
canoeing;

In helping those who really need,
In giving food to those whom you can feed.

Thank God for all you have and had:
For the happy moments and the ones which were sad.

Because He loves you.
He wants you to be happy and to succeed, oh how much it is
true!

*Wednesday*                    *18.03.2015*

# Church

Church is the only place
Where you are always welcome, friend.
Whether you are fast or slow, come at your own pace;
Whatever happened, come, God can mend.

*Sunday*                                      *17.01.2016*

# Only lazy people can't fly

Only lazy people can't fly
Because an Orthodox prayer is like a wing.
In doubt? Then you should try:
Thank for all, repent, and ask; pray in silence or sing.

*Wednesday – Friday*                    *06-08.01.2016*

# Up vector

I have been running from believing,
Trying to find happiness elsewhere
Losing things instead of receiving
And found happiness nowhere.

The more I live, the more I see –
There is one way:
Up and it is free;
To choose love in all situations, to pray.
*Saturday*                              *28.11.2015*

# Veterans

They gave their lives
That we may enjoy the things we like.
Due to them peace thrives;
Without fear I can ride my bike.

Thank you
For you have showed courage, faith, and love.
You have prepared the place for the peace dove.
Every day you stood to your duty anew.

We remember and pray for you.
We live because your courageous deeds were true.
We enjoy hockey, pancakes, maple syrup, and barbecue.
Your glory did not fade, it grew.

*Wednesday*                    *11.11.2015*


# Space exploration

A lot has been done in terms of exploration of space,
But much more remains to be done at a confident pace.
Space hides secrets which can help us,
We should proceed without much fuss.

Other social programs are important too,
But space is just another social thing which is true.
So, let's continue exploring,
Let us avoid worrying.

Did you know that every cent invested
Returns twenty when projects in space are tested?
Space exploration and social programs should go hand in hand;
Space exploration should benefit people, animals, air, water, and
land.

*Wednesday*                            *11.11.2015*


# Never let your praying knees get lazy

Never let your praying knees get lazy.
Add love to all the things you do.
Let your words be as beautiful and simple as a daisy.
Let the things you say be true.

Be polite, hold the door, say thank you at once.
When you are wrong, apologize.
This may be hard at first glance,
But this will help you to awesomize.

*Saturday*                            *07.11.2015*


# Everybody needs time to be alone

Everybody needs time to be alone:
Without friends, without noise, without a phone.
Everybody needs time to pray –
To speak with God, to reflect on His way.
*Sunday*                            *11.10.2015*

# Life of a modern scholar

What is life of a modern scholar like?
He (let us use masculine for the purpose of convenience)
Gets up, brushes teeth, drinks water, prays, and rides his bike.
He does not start his day with scholarly opinions.

He returns from his workout,
Takes shower, if required,
Has his breakfast, sometimes with sauerkraut.
He does not start work until after meal to avoid being tired.

When the meal is done,
It's time to tackle tasks;
But for lunch he is gone
To eat, to rest, to prepare to answer whatever his class asks.

When his work (research and classes)
Is done for the day,
He puts away bulbs and weird masses,
He returns home without delay.

He has his dinner before six o'clock.
This meal is lightest, lunch is mid,
Breakfast is heartiest – this rule is like a rock.
He rejoices over what he did.

Besides his usual things,
He goes to a swimming pool twice a week.
He goes to Church on Sunday        to share prayer and what the
Lord graciously gives.
He makes healthy food, he is meek.

He likes reading books about adventures,
Enjoys spending time with family and friends.
He does charity and other worthy ventures.
At 9pm his day ends.

He goes to bed at this time.
He prays, brushes teeth, washes his face.
This scholar likes wise and harmless rhyme.
Things in life are to be taken at a moderate pace.

*Thursday*                    *29.10.2015*


# There is time for all

There is time to work
And there is time to play;
Time to eat pork
And time to "vegetize" your tray.

There is time to cry
And there is time to smile;
Time to refrain and time to try;
To rest and to cover a mile.

*Sunday*                    *11.10.2015*

# Have you every felt?

Have you ever felt really bad
When you're all fingers and thumbs and look so sad?
I think you have, perhaps not once.
Perhaps you even asked God to help you not to lose your chance.

It's very good when you believe;
This opens the door to wisdom which you receive.
Never forget to thank for what you've got.
Look at paupers, think carefully – you have a lot.

Have you ever had bright moments in life
When the sky is clear and you want to fife?..
Be thankful to score your goal!
Ask God to show the way and to save your soul.

*Monday*                    *11.07.2005*


# My emotions are a part of me

My emotions are a part of me,
Just like a book and its page;
A leaf isn't stronger than the whole tree
And feelings need no cage.

Bad emotions will be out of court,
That is I'm gonna exchange them for good ones;
God's help, a sincere smile will be my support.
Bad emotions will disappear faster than the cheetah runs.
*Friday*                              *01.07.2005*

# Language is a well of knowledge

Language is a well of knowledge.
It is spoken and also studied at college.
I use it everyday and everywhere,
But I've never looked at it with due care.

I've been studying it since school,
But even now I can't remember each rule.
Language is like a puzzle
And here even a dog won't nuzzle.

God gave us this gift.
The gift is powerful, fair, and has no sift.
With language one can bring in pleasure
Or sorrow if he doesn't want or doesn't see the measure.

The language is also like an ocean:
It's deep, full of good things and is always in motion.
We need it like grass needs dew.
Thanks to language I write; thanks to it I speak to You.

*Saturday*                    *25.06.2005*


# Patience is a virtue

Patience is a virtue,
The lack of it can hurt you.
A person who can possess himself and is witty
Is better than the one who can capture a city.

You can have an army and money,
But this will not make your day sunny;
And they can disappear quickly; –
Cover yourself with wisdom and patience thickly.

The beginning of wisdom is the fear of God, truly.
Cheer up, have faith and act duly.
Have patience on all the paths of life:
At work, at school, with your husband or wife.

*Sunday – Thursday*                    *24-28.05.2015*


# Blessed is the man that has the fear of God truly

Blessed is the man that has the fear of God truly,
That delights in His commandments and performs them fully.
His seed will be mighty on earth all over;
His house will thrive, his cattle will have ample clover.

*Friday*                    *29.05.2015*


# Environment

Our environment is our home.
Nature is fragile and needs protection.
We get food and all we need under its dome,
But today it is in a state which requires a decisive action.

Wars, transportation, air pollution,
Empoisoned agriculture...
These things require a wise solution.
Man is a reason-endowed creature, not a dumb vulture.

First we need to control our appetite,
Then we should develop alternative ways –
Each of us can make his/her impact light.
We should act fast – within hours, not within days.

*Saturday*                                    *12.09.2015*


# I hope you'll never lose the sense of wonder

I hope you'll never lose the sense of wonder –
After a lot of rain and thunder –
You will remember to hope
And believe that with God's help, somehow you'll cope.

I hope you will sing –
Without being afraid of what kind of thing
People will think or say –
Because you are like a sun ray.

I hope you will dance –
Without being afraid of giving a chance
Of saying that you are awkward or old –
Let the joyful child in you always live, let your heart never
become stone-cold.

*Thursday*                                    *16.07.2015*

# For driving

When you drive, drive in a way which is safe and sure.
If unsure, don't go.
You will save a life, the baby will enjoy the sky azure.
Your payments on your car will be so low.

When you use your car, make safe your drive.
It happens that out of nowhere cars and people dive,
But you be cautious at all times
With yourself and others to save precious lives.

*Friday*                    *21.08.2015*


# Blueberry

Blueberry! What a delicious thing!
If you go to visit a friend, that's the best thing to bring!
It is rich in antioxidants and healthy all over
With tart, sweet taste and gentle scent as freshly cut clover.

*Friday*                    *14.08.2015*


# Temple of food

There is a temple of food
Right in the centre of a city.
People go there, but it does no good,
It's a pity.

Only to those it does good
Who go there for minutes, not for good.
Good is in good, not in food.
This is how I would like to conclude.

*Saturday*                    *02.07.2011*


# Communicate

Your sacrifice can be communication
And be ready to offer it,
At work or at vacation,
It can help your neighbour out of a pit.

It can simply provoke a kind smile
And you'll improve your neighbour's mood.
Together or individually, you'll cover a thoushand's mile.
Communication makes your soul good.

*Sunday – Monday*              *28-29.08.2011*


# Acquisition of the Holy Spirit

The fast and the prayer are not ultimate goals;
The aim is acquisition of the Holy Spirit indeed.
The Holy Spirit comforts our souls
And works to remove every weed.

But the fast and the prayer are wings
Bringing us closer to God in any situation.
The Holy Spirit helps us to find all the good things.
Acquire the Holy Spirit regardless of where you were born,
when, and to what nation.

*Friday*                              *10.07.2015*


# Once upon a time

Once a man committed a crime:
He stole something at that time.
Then the police were on his trail.
The man was spotted by a friar.

The latter took him to his monastery cell
And treated his wounds very well.
When the police came after their prey,
The monk did not betray.

Since then the man often prayed
And both souls were saved.

*Sunday*                              *05.08.2012*


# Do good till you have strength to do so

Do good till you have strength to do so!
Two, three or more times in a row

And let your own business thrive
Because God gives and does not deprive.

Start now and patient be,
Let good health be granted to thee.
When in hardships, let us pray.
Let's do good things without delay!

*Sunday – Monday*                    *13-14.05.2012*

# Be consistent in good

Be consistent in good:
Do something good all the time!
For our souls, kind things are like food;
So, nourish it well with kind deeds and good rhyme.

Watch what you say,
Be patient when people are rude
'Cause you have your own way.
Whatever they do, try to do things which are good!

*Thursday*                    *11.12.2014*

# A kind smile can heal

A kind smile can heal,
More than that: it cures for sure.

People will smile back whatever they feel.
It's true in space, underground, at sea, and ashore.

Good mood passes over to people around.
Even if they are unhappy, suppressed,
They hear the jolly sound
And bad mood disappears without rest.

So, try to smile at your neighbour.
Believe! You need no hesitation,
And he will help you back with your labour.
Language of good needs no translation!

*Sunday*                              *18.11.2007*

# Index (tags)

*Літературно-художнє видання*
# Ярослав Вайз

# Радійте!
Лірика
Англійською мовою

Підписано до друку 12.04.2019 р.
Формат 60x84 1/16. Папір офсетний.
Гарнітура «Times»
Друк RISO. Ум. друк. арк. 16,74
Обл. вид. арк. 16,97.
Наклад 140 прим. Зам. 591

Видано та виготовлено
Видавець ФО-П Стасюк Л.С.
м.Хмельницький, вул.Дубініна, 6/2.
тел. 180978557497
E-mail: lilia_stasuk@i.ua
www.vidatiknigu.com.ua
Свідоцтво про внесення суб'єкта видавничої справи
до державного реєстру видавців, виготівників
та розповсюджувачів видавничої продукції
Серія ДК №4270 від 22.02.2012 р.